WILLIAMS-SONOMA

MASTERING

Soups & Stews

Author
MARIE SIMMONS

General Editor
CHUCK WILLIAMS

Photographer
JEFF KAUCK

NEW YORK · LONDON · TORONTO · SYDNEY

Mastering Soups & Stews offers every reader a cooking class in book form, a one-on-one lesson with a seasoned teacher standing by your side, explaining each recipe step-by-step—with plenty of photographs to illustrate every detail.

Soup is among the most appreciated item on any menu, and learning how to make soups will arm you with invaluable kitchen skills. For example, once you have made cream of broccoli soup a few times, you'll have the know-how to cook many other soups. In the pages that follow, you'll discover this and other classic recipes with user-friendly explanations for techniques that transform everyday ingredients into the soups and stews everyone enjoys.

In the opening pages, you'll find a brief overview of what's ahead, information on various types of soups and stews, and tips on ingredients and on cooking, seasoning, and serving soups and stews. Next comes the Basic Recipes chapter, which includes detailed instructions for half a dozen stocks, the building blocks of many soups and stews and other dishes. If you encounter a direction that you don't understand, you can turn to the section on Key Techniques, where easy-to-follow text and photographs teach fundamental techniques, such as how to slice carrots, peel and dice onions, or prepare shellfish. Finally, the recipes are divided into four categories: clear soups, puréed soups, cream soups & chowders, and stews. As you progress to more sophisticated dishes, you will continue to acquire skills and insight, such as the best ways to purée soups, how to thicken soups and stews, and the secret of browning meats.

So, let's get started: Fill your stockpot with a chicken, some vegetables, and water and bring everything to a gentle boil. You are now on your way to making the first of many great soups.

Chuck Williams

Working with the Recipes

Think of your kitchen as a cooking school and this book as the all-wise instructor, always available to offer advice or demonstrate a technique when you need help, from how to seed and dice a tomato to how to purée a soup using a blender. Each recipe provides a set of easy-to-follow instructions that produce a memorable soup every time. Always read a recipe carefully, visualizing each step as if you are watching an accomplished cooking teacher at work.

Learning to cook starts with becoming adept at a basic skill and then using it until it becomes second nature. To make soups and stews, the first thing you need to know is how to cook the chicken, beef, vegetable, and seafood stocks on which they are based, which are found here in the Basic Recipes chapter. Indeed, such stocks are the foundation of many dishes beyond soups. Master them and you're on your way to becoming a great cook.

Each subsequent chapter starts with at least one master recipe, which takes you through a classic soup recipe step-by-step, with both words and pictures. I suggest tackling these key skill-building recipes first. You'll find it's like having a cooking teacher in the kitchen with you as you work.

After you have practiced the master recipes, the other recipes will help you continue your learning. Secure in the skills you have developed in the master recipes, and guided by photos illustrating any confusing or difficult aspects of the other recipes, your soup-making confidence will steadily increase as you progress through the book.

Recipe variations provide another way to hone your cooking expertise and build a solid repertory of soup recipes. For example, once you learn how to make Chicken Soup (page 47) you'll have the skills necessary to make Matzoh Ball Soup (page 53) and Asian Chicken Soup (page 53) by changing a few ingredients.

To find out more about the basic tools and equipment you will need to make these recipes, turn to pages 132–35.

Types of Soups & Stews

Some of the world's best-loved dishes are soups and stews. Think of the minestrone of Italy and the bouillabaisse of France's southern coast—one a cornucopia of vegetables, the other a kettle brimming with seafood. Part of their appeal is their unique flavors, but it is also the homey warmth that they bring to a table surrounded by friends and family. Although soups and stews share these two important traits, they are also defined by their differences.

Soups can be classified according to the liquid used as the base, and also by the manner in which subsequent additions are treated. This book is divided into four chapters, according to these distinctions.

Clear Soups

Clear soups require a patiently simmered and carefully skimmed stock. Typically, clear soups feature this clear, flavorful liquid brimming with meat or vegetables, as in Chicken Soup (page 47). But French Onion Soup (page 55) is also considered a clear soup. Although an abundance of caramelized onions and a topping of toasted bread and melted cheese may obscure that fact, onion soup begins with a clear beef stock.

Puréed Soups

Despite the fact that puréed soups also typically rely on a clear stock, their character is defined instead by the vegetables they contain. Carrots, leeks, tomatoes, potatoes, dried beans—each separately or in combination—can be cooked in stock and then puréed to make a smooth soup, or only part can be puréed to create a pleasing contrast of chunky ingredients in a smooth base.

Cream Soups & Chowders

Cream soups form a natural alliance with chowders and bisques, as most of them depend on the addition of milk or cream for their signature richness. Classic cream soups, such as Cream of Broccoli Soup (page 93), begin with a butter-and-flour roux that acts as a thickener and are finished with heavy (double) cream for a silky texture. Chowders, most often chunky mixtures, usually contain potatoes and onions along with other vegetables or seafood and a smoky hint of bacon.

The term *bisque* was originally applied only to smooth, cream-based seafood soups made with lobster, shrimp (prawns), crab, or crayfish. However, now it is often used to describe any thick, creamy-rich, smooth soup. Cooked rice, although not always used, is a traditional thickener for bisque.

Stews

Stews generally contain bite-sized bits of meat, seafood, or vegetables in a saucelike broth. They are versatile, utilizing tough but flavorful cuts of meat, dried beans, or grains such as pasta. Meat stews are typically cooked for a long time to tenderize the meat and marry all the flavors. Shellfish stews, such as Bouillabaisse (page 119), are cooked relatively briefly to preserve the fresh flavor and texture of their more delicate ingredients.

Understanding Soup & Stew Ingredients

Soup or stew, no matter how skillfully you cook it, can only be as good as the ingredients you use to make it. Freshness is always important, so when you shop, learn to recognize whether the chicken or seafood, leafy greens or herbs are at their best before you buy them. Many staple foods are always available, of course, but some vegetables and seafood are at their finest during a brief season. Purchase them at their peak for superior flavor.

Stock Ingredients

You may already know that making a memorable soup depends on using a full-bodied, full-flavored chicken, beef, fish, shellfish, or vegetable stock. All of these stocks can be made in advance, cooled, and stored in the refrigerator or freezer, where they sit ready to bring savor to a variety of soups.

While homemade stock makes the best soups and stews, there may be occasions when you don't have the time to make a stock from scratch or have no frozen stock on hand. Experienced cooks rely on just-made stocks, available in plastic containers, from specialty-food stores or upscale markets. A can or aseptic carton of low-sodium broth can also be used to make soups and stews, but it's best to augment it with a few fresh ingredients to brighten the flavor: Pour the broth into a pan, add an equal amount of water, ½ pound (250 g) chicken or beef bones, and a chopped onion or carrot, if desired. Bring to a boil, skim off the foam, and then simmer for about an hour.

When you use commercial stocks, be wary of adding extra salt, as they might already be salty enough. At each stage of preparation, taste the soup, and don't add the salt called for in the recipe unless you think it's needed.

Meats, Poultry & Seafood

The cuts that make the richest soups and stews originate in bony and less tender parts of the animal—beef marrowbones and shins, lamb shoulder or neck. If you don't see them in your butcher's case, ask

for them. If they're not in stock, they may be available by special order. If not, discuss your needs and let the butcher suggest a practical substitution.

Purchasing a cut-up chicken is a time-saver, and specific chicken parts are convenient for some recipes. When you make Chicken Stock (page 18), however, you'll want to go for the boniest cuts. Backs and necks are ideal. Some cooks set them aside when they carve a roast chicken and save them in the freezer until they're ready to make stock. For most soup making, a whole chicken is your best bet. Cooking a whole bird in stock results in an unbeatable flavor.

Fish and shellfish must be fresh for the best flavor. Seafood should smell of salty sea air. Don't buy it if it has a fishy odor. Not all fish markets display the heads and frames you need for Fish Stock

(page 26), but a request will often produce them. Shrimp (prawns) should be firm and smell faintly sweet, while tightly closed shells indicate that clams and mussels are alive and fresh (an open shell should close when tapped gently).

Vegetables

A quintet of vegetables is indispensable for many soups and stews: onions, garlic, shallots, carrots, and celery. Fortunately, the first three are sturdy enough to store at cool room temperature, while the other two can linger for a week or so in the refrigerator.

Beyond these necessities, let the seasons dictate your vegetable selection. Artichokes, asparagus, and English peas are ideal candidates for spring soups. Midsummer, when tomatoes are at their most flavorful, is the best time to make

Gazpacho (page 88). Tomato Soup (page 77), in contrast, is more versatile. You can make it with either fresh or quality canned tomatoes, depending on the time of year.

Because hot soup and stew are popular cold-weather choices, you'll find that many are based on the stars of the fall and winter harvest, such as potatoes, Swiss chard, beets, and winter squashes.

Herbs & Spices

The subtle flavors in a soup or stew come from the ingredients you add most sparingly: herbs and spices. Use fresh herbs whenever possible and wash them thoroughly before using. Dried herbs and spices should be used within six months of purchase, as they lose flavor with age. Freshly ground spices, including pepper, will give the best-tasting results.

Cooking and Seasoning Soups & Stews

In learning to make soups and stews, you'll discover one of the fundamental secrets of the kitchen: long, slow cooking transforms ordinary ingredients into flavorful, satisfying dishes. Although some soups and stews need to simmer for a while, they adapt smoothly to a busy schedule. They are also good candidates for making in ample quantities in advance and refrigerating or freezing. Often this resting period improves flavor.

Using Your Senses

Cooking soups and stews engages all your senses. When you bring a kettle of chicken parts, water, vegetables, and seasonings to a boil, you will see the water tremble, then hear it churn to a full boil. As heat coaxes aromas from the ingredients, you will smell their fragrance. You will test the doneness of meat and vegetables by how tender they feel as you bite into a piece or pierce it with a fork.

When you make stock, bring it to a boil slowly and watch carefully. When big, active bubbles come to the surface, reduce the heat at once. Your goal is a steady simmer, with small bubbles occasionally rising to the surface.

Stock should not be stirred as it simmers, as that will make it cloudy. Instead, using a large spoon, skim the stock at regular intervals to remove the impurities that rise to the surface. Simmering soups and stews, however, should be stirred occasionally to help distribute flavorful elements. Stirring

also lets you know if anything is sticking to the pan—a sign to reduce the heat. If you're not sure whether you are supposed to stir or not, double-check the recipe.

Vegetable Cuts for Soup

Slicing or chopping ingredients uniformly contributes to even cooking, so recipes are specific about how to cut soup vegetables. Potatoes of the same size and shape, for example, cook in the same amount of time. The way you cut the ingredients also affects the soup's flavor. A sliced carrot exposes two surfaces to the simmering stock. But if you chop the slices, you expose even more surface area, contributing additional flavor to the simmering liquid.

Using Seasonings Wisely

Seasonings, the ingredients you usually add by the teaspoonful or a few leaves at a time, transform a soup or stew in subtle but important ways. Leafy herbs—usually bay leaf, parsley, and thyme—tied with kitchen string in a square of cheesecloth

(muslin) are known as a *bouquet garni* in classic French cooking. Included this way, the herbs season a stock without crumbling, do not interfere with skimming, and are easily removed. (If you do not have cheesecloth or kitchen string on hand, you can slip the herbs into a teaball.)

The more stocks, soups, and stews you make, the better you will understand how and when to adjust seasonings. Seasoning a soup or stew depends on your personal preference; the seasoning ingredients called for in the recipes are only suggestions. In the end, the final flavor of a dish is really your decision. The recipe is only a guide.

Taste as you cook, and you will begin to appreciate how a technique like *sweating*—cooking vegetables in oil or butter over low heat until they are soft—releases more flavor than adding the same ingredients raw.

Browning meat, whether you roast beef bones for Brown Beef Stock (page 22), or cook cubes of beef in oil for Chili con

Carne (page 128), produces a richer flavor than simply simmering the beef in stock or water.

Salt is the most basic ingredient, yet when and how you add it affects the flavor of foods significantly. A sprinkle of salt brightens a soup's flavor, while a salt brine makes poultry juicy and tender.

If you finish cooking a soup and the final flavor seems dull to you, consider other ingredients. For example, lemon juice is an outstanding accent for seafood and vegetable soups. Freshly ground pepper or nutmeg or a splash of dry sherry can heighten the flavor of a cream soup. Drizzle in a little balsamic vinegar to perk up a meat stew.

Thickening Soups & Stews

Soup tastes better if it feels good in your mouth. A satisfying soup should be neither too thin, nor too dense. There are several ways to perfect consistency, depending on the nature of the dish. Sometimes it's as simple as puréeing some or all of the vegetables, using a blender, food processor, immersion blender, or food mill. Each recipe in this book specifies the best tool for the job. For other recipes, you'll learn when to bring a cooked mixture together with a thickener, such as a *roux* (flour cooked in oil or butter), puréed vegetables, or rice. Each affects flavor, consistency, and the clarity of the soup differently, and each recipe will lead you to the right choice.

If a soup thickens too much, stir in more stock, a tablespoon or two at a time, to correct the texture. Milk can be used to thin a cream soup. And sometimes all it takes to improve an over-rich stew is a little warm water.

Food Safety

Putting hot items directly in the refrigerator raises the temperature of the other foods stored there, which can lead to spoilage. Before refrigerating hot soup or stock, rapidly cool it to room temperature to prevent bacterial growth: Place hot stock or soup in a metal or tempered glass bowl, then put it in another bowl partially filled with water and ice cubes. Stir the soup frequently to speed cooling. When the soup is at least lukewarm, transfer it to storage containers and refrigerate or freeze. Affix a label with the recipe name and date.

Serving Soups & Stews

When you've worked long and hard to create a flavorful soup or stew, it's important to think about the best way to serve it. Throughout this book, you'll find suggestions for finishing touches that will help you do just that. You'll discover that with little extra effort you can bring a touch of style and additional flavor to your soups and stews. You can also apply many of these same easy garnishing ideas to other dishes that you make.

In some restaurants, garnishes are overused to the point of absurdity, but you don't need to fall into that trap. Instead, think of how to make your garnishes both eye-catching and delicious. Creative garnishes can either echo or contrast with the flavors, colors, and textures in the dish they embellish.

Remember that a garnish should always be edible. For example, save snippets of thyme to scatter over the topping of French Onion Soup (page 59), or fry a few sage leaves to adorn White Bean Soup (page 85). Crème fraîche or yogurt can be used to create an appealing flourish on bowls of a puréed soup, such as Carrot-Ginger Soup (page 73). An easy way to garnish a cream-based vegetable soup is to set aside a few small pieces of the vegetable before puréeing and use them to top bowls of the finished soup. You'll see this treatment in Cream of Broccoli Soup (page 97). Finally, sauté bread cubes briefly in olive oil to make crunchy croutons to top a variety of soups.

Warming & Chilling Bowls

A welcome touch is to serve hot soups and stews in warmed bowls. Slip the bowls into a 200°F (95°C) oven for about 15 minutes to warm through. By the same token, a chilled soup will retain its optimal serving temperature longer if ladled into bowls that have spent at least 10 minutes in the refrigerator.

Measuring Ingredients

Before you start any recipe, remember to measure out all your ingredients. While some noted cooks appear to have a nonchalant attitude about measurements, the "I'll just add a little bit of cream" school of cooking is ill-suited to the inexperienced and can be disastrous. Until you've cooked enough to have developed a reliable sense of quantities, you will achieve much better results by using the standard measurements found in the recipes that follow.

Mise en Place

Preparing and measuring the ingredients you'll need for a recipe and assembling them ahead of time is known by the French term *mise en place*, meaning "everything in its place." Get in the habit of doing this, even if it seems like a lot of extra work. In the end, your time in the kitchen will go more smoothly.

It's helpful to have small bowls or ramekins for holding the chopped and/or measured ingredients, all ready to add when directed in a recipe. Before you begin to assemble the ingredients, give the recipe a careful read. Recipes in this book are specific about when ingredients need to be prepared. Often you'll find you don't need everything in the ingredient list at once. When making Shrimp Bisque (page 105), for example, while the stock simmers, you can prepare the ingredients for the bisque base.

Dry Ingredients

Many standard soup ingredients, such as onions, carrots, and celery, are given here in their naturally occurring forms (a large onion or carrot), but for greater precision in some recipes, measurements for these and other nonliquid ingredients are given in cups. When you measure 1 cup orzo or ½ cup chopped fresh basil for Minestrone (page 61), you'll need a set of measuring cups. Made of either metal or plastic, dry measuring cups generally come in a set of four (¼ cup, ⅓ cup, ½ cup, 1 cup).

To measure, fill the cup of the specified size to the top; level off the contents, if necessary, using the straight edge of a knife or spatula. When you are working with light ingredients such as basil leaves, chopped parsley, or grated cheese, you may be directed to pack them lightly to achieve an accurate measurement.

Liquid Ingredients

Liquid ingredients require another type of measuring cup, one that can be easily filled and poured from without spilling. The cups of clear tempered glass or clear plastic are made in a variety of sizes, ranging from 1 cup (8 fl oz/250 ml) to 2 quarts (2 l) or more. Soups and stews usually require large quantities of stock and other liquid, so it's convenient to have not only a 1-cup measure but also some larger sizes. To measure liquids accurately, pour in the indicated amount and then check at eye level.

Small Measurements

For small quantities of dry and liquid ingredients, ¼ cup or less, equip your kitchen with a set of measuring spoons (¼ teaspoon, ½ teaspoon, 1 teaspoon, 1 tablespoon). Metal spoons hold up best through repeated washings.

1

Basic Recipes

Learning how to prepare stocks is one of the first lessons in any basic cooking class, and feeling confident making them is especially important when cooking soups and stews. In this chapter, you will find out how to work with the meat, poultry, and fish bones that go into stocks and how to simmer, skim, and defat stocks to ensure a clean, clear taste and appearance.

Chicken Stock

Chicken stock is a staple ingredient for many soups and stews. Although there are many good stocks available commercially, homemade stock is still the best for the flavor and body it gives to a soup. The good news is that you can make the stock in double or triple batches and then freeze it until you need it.

1 large carrot

1 large stalk celery with leaves

1 clove garlic

1 large or 2 medium yellow onions

6 lb (3 kg) chicken backs and necks

3 or 4 sprigs fresh flat-leaf (Italian) parsley

1 bay leaf

8–10 peppercorns

MAKES ABOUT 4 QT (4 L)

1 Cut the vegetables

Peel the carrot, then cut it into 1-inch (2.5-cm) lengths. Cut the celery into the same-sized pieces as the carrot. Next, peel the garlic, but leave the clove whole. Finally, peel the onion, then quarter it through the stem end.

2 Bring the stock to a boil

Place the chicken, carrot, celery, garlic clove, onion quarters, parsley, bay leaf, and peppercorns in an 8-qt (8-l) heavy-bottomed pot and add water just to cover the ingredients by 1 inch (2.5 cm); more water could dilute the flavor of the stock. Place the pot over medium-high heat. Without stirring, slowly bring the liquid to a boil.

3 Simmer the stock

As soon as you see large bubbles begin to form, reduce the heat until only small bubbles occasionally break the surface of the liquid. Use a skimmer or a large slotted spoon to skim the grayish foam that rises to the surface of the liquid for the first 10 minutes of cooking. The foam is the result of collagen and gelatin being released from the bones and meat; if it's not removed, it will cloud the stock. Continue to simmer the stock, uncovered, adjusting the heat periodically to keep the stock at a gentle simmer, for 2–2½ hours. Do not stir, but continue to skim the surface every 30 minutes or so. Add more water, if necessary, to keep the ingredients just covered.

4 **Strain the stock**

Cut a piece of cheesecloth (muslin) large enough to line the inside of a fine-mesh sieve when it is triple layered. Fold the cheesecloth, dampen it with cool water, squeeze it dry, then use it to line the sieve. Place the sieve over a large tempered-glass or stainless-steel bowl. Remove the larger solids with the skimmer or slotted spoon and then ladle or carefully pour the stock through the sieve. Discard the solids that are in the sieve.

5 **Defat or cool the stock**

Before you use the stock, carefully remove all of the fat, or the soups made from the stock will have a greasy flavor and texture. Use a large metal spoon to skim the clear yellow fat from the surface of the strained stock. Or, if time allows, chill the stock before defatting. Fill a large bowl partway with ice water and set the bowl of stock in the ice bath to cool it to room temperature, stirring occasionally. Cover and refrigerate the stock overnight. The fat will rise to the top and solidify, making it easy to lift off the surface.

6 **Store the stock**

Cover and refrigerate the stock if you plan to use it within 3 days, or ladle or pour it into airtight containers, filling them to within about ½ inch (12 mm) of the rim (the stock expands as it freezes), and freeze for up to 3 months. To thaw frozen stock, refrigerate for 24 hours, or transfer the frozen block of stock to a saucepan and melt slowly over low heat, covered, until liquefied. Then, measure the amount needed for the recipes.

CHEF'S TIP

Some chefs prefer to bundle some of the aromatic ingredients into a square of damp cheesecloth (muslin) secured with kitchen string. This bouquet garni *keeps the aromatic ingredients, such as herb sprigs, bay leaves, and leafy celery tops, from floating in the stock and interfering with the skimming process.*

Beef Stock

A generous mix of marrowbones and beef shins, two cuts good butchers traditionally carry, gives your beef stock a distinctive and aromatic, yet mild flavor and light body. Ending up with a perfectly clear liquid is important, too, which you achieve with careful cooking, straining, and defatting.

2 large carrots

2 stalks celery with leaves

1 large yellow onion

3 lb (1.5 kg) beef marrowbones, cracked by the butcher

2 thick slices meaty beef shin, about 2 lb (1 kg) total weight

3 or 4 sprigs fresh flat-leaf (Italian) parsley

1 bay leaf

8–10 peppercorns

MAKES ABOUT 2 QT (2 L)

1 Cut the vegetables

Peel the carrots, then cut them on the diagonal into ½-inch (12-mm) pieces. Cut the celery into pieces the same size as the carrots. Next, peel the onion, and then cut it into 1-inch (2.5-cm) cubes.

2 Bring the stock to a boil

Place the marrowbones and beef shin in an 8-qt (8-l) heavy-bottomed pot. Add the carrots, celery, onion, parsley, bay leaf, and peppercorns and add water just to cover the ingredients by 1 inch (2.5 cm); more water could dilute the flavor of the stock. Place the pot over medium-high heat. Without stirring, slowly bring the liquid to a boil.

3 Simmer the stock

As soon as you see large bubbles begin to form, reduce the heat until only small bubbles occasionally break the surface of the liquid. Use a large slotted spoon or skimmer to skim the grayish foam that rises to the surface of the liquid for the first 10 minutes of cooking. The foam is the result of collagen and gelatin being released from the bones and meat; if it's not removed, it will cloud the stock. Continue to simmer the stock, uncovered, adjusting the heat periodically to keep the stock at a gentle simmer, for 3–4 hours. Do not stir, but continue to skim the surface every 30 minutes or so. Add more water, if necessary, to keep the ingredients just covered. Remove the larger solids with the slotted spoon or a sieve before straining the stock.

Strain the stock

4 Cut a piece of cheesecloth (muslin) large enough to line the inside of a fine-mesh sieve when it is triple layered. Fold the cheesecloth, dampen it with cool water, squeeze it dry, then use it to line the sieve. Place the sieve over a large tempered-glass or stainless-steel bowl and then ladle or carefully pour the stock through the sieve. Discard the solids that are in the sieve.

Defat or cool the stock

5 Before you use the stock, carefully remove all of the fat, or the soups made from the stock will have a greasy flavor and texture. Use a large metal spoon to skim the clear yellow fat from the surface of the strained stock. Or, if time allows, chill the stock before defatting. Fill a large bowl partway with ice water and set the bowl of stock in the ice bath to cool it to room temperature, stirring occasionally. Cover, pour into an airtight container, and refrigerate the stock overnight. The fat will rise to the top and solidify, making it easy to lift off the surface.

Store the stock

6 Cover and refrigerate the stock if you plan to use it within 3 days, or ladle or pour it into airtight containers, filling them to within about ½ inch (12 mm) of the rim (the stock expands as it freezes), and freeze for up to 3 months. To thaw frozen stock, refrigerate for 24 hours, or transfer the frozen block of stock to a saucepan and melt slowly over low heat, covered, until liquefied. Then, measure the amount needed for the recipes.

CHEF'S TIP

When the stock is ready, some chefs like to remove the pot from the heat to a turned-off burner and let the stock stand for about 30 minutes before straining. During this standing period, the solids settle to the bottom of the pot and the stock cools slightly, making it easier and safer to strain.

Brown Beef Stock

Some hearty soups and stews call for a particularly deep, rich stock. This can be achieved by initially browning the meats and vegetables in the oven, which causes the meat juices to form a glaze and the natural sugars in the vegetables to caramelize, imparting extra body and flavor to the finished stock.

2 large carrots

2 stalks celery with leaves

1 large yellow onion

Canola oil for preparing the pan

3 lb (1.5 kg) beef marrowbones, cracked by the butcher

2 thick slices meaty beef shin, about 2 lb (1 kg) total weight

2 cups (16 fl oz/500 ml) water, plus more to cover the ingredients

3 or 4 sprigs fresh flat-leaf (Italian) parsley

1 bay leaf

8–10 peppercorns

MAKES ABOUT 2 QT (2 L)

1 Cut the vegetables

Peel the carrots, then cut them on the diagonal into ½-inch (12-mm) pieces. Cut the celery into pieces the same size as the carrots. Next, peel the onion, and then cut it into 1-inch (2.5-cm) cubes.

2 Brown the bones and vegetables

Position a rack in the upper third of the oven and preheat to 400°F (200°C). Lightly oil a large roasting pan. Spread the marrowbones, beef shin, carrots, celery, and onion in the pan. Roast, turning the meats and vegetables once or twice, until all the ingredients are a deep mahogany brown, about 45 minutes.

3 Deglaze the roasting pan

Using tongs, transfer the meat and the vegetables to an 8-qt (8-l) heavy-bottomed pot. Protecting your hand with an oven mitt, tip the roasting pan to gather the fat at one corner. Use a spoon to remove the clear fat. Place the roasting pan on the stove top over 2 burners, turn on the heat to low, and add the 2 cups water. Using a wide wooden spatula, scrape up the dark bits of juices that have cooked onto the bottom of the pan and stir to dissolve them in the water. This technique, called *deglazing*, is important because it adds a deep caramelized flavor and rich amber color to the finished stock.

4 Bring the stock to a boil

Pour the contents of the roasting pan into the pot holding the browned ingredients. Add the parsley, bay leaf, and peppercorns to the pot. Add water just to cover the ingredients by 1 inch (2.5 cm); more water could dilute the flavor. Place the pot over medium-high heat. Without stirring, slowly bring the liquid to a boil.

5 Simmer the stock

As soon as you see large bubbles begin to form, reduce the heat until only small bubbles occasionally break the surface of the liquid. Use a large slotted spoon or skimmer to skim the grayish foam that rises to the surface of the liquid for the first 10 minutes of cooking. The foam is the result of collagen and gelatin being released from the bones and meat; if it's not removed, it will cloud the stock. Continue to simmer the stock, uncovered, adjusting the heat periodically to keep the stock at a gentle simmer, for 3–4 hours. Do not stir, but continue to skim the surface every 30 minutes or so. Add more water, if necessary, to keep the ingredients just covered.

6 Strain the stock

Cut a piece of cheesecloth (muslin) large enough to line the inside of a fine-mesh sieve when it is triple layered. Fold the cheesecloth, dampen it with cool water, squeeze it dry, then use it to line the sieve. Place the sieve over a large tempered-glass or stainless-steel bowl. Remove the larger solids and then ladle or carefully pour the stock through the sieve. Discard the solids that are in the sieve.

7 Defat or cool the stock

Before you use the stock, carefully remove all of the fat, or the soups made from the stock will have a greasy flavor and texture. Use a large metal spoon to skim the clear yellow fat from the surface of the strained stock. Or, if time allows, chill the stock before defatting. Fill a large bowl partway with ice water and set the bowl of stock in the ice bath to cool it to room temperature, stirring occasionally. Cover and refrigerate the stock overnight. The fat will rise to the top and solidify, making it easy to lift off the surface.

8 Store the stock

Cover and refrigerate the stock if you plan to use it within 3 days, or ladle or pour it into airtight containers, and freeze for up to 3 months. To thaw, transfer the frozen stock to a saucepan and melt slowly over low heat, covered, until liquefied. Then, measure the amount needed for the recipe.

CHEF'S TIP

I like to put the bowls and sieve in the sink before straining stock. Because the sink is lower than the countertop, working there makes it easier to transfer the stock to the sieve. It also simplifies cleanup if there are drips.

2 or 3 medium yellow onions

3 or 4 carrots

6 oz (185 g) fresh white mushrooms

1 small leek, white and pale green parts

1 red bell pepper (capsicum)

2 tomatoes

2 or 3 stalks celery with leaves

1 small turnip

1 small parsnip

4 cloves garlic

2 tablespoons extra-virgin olive oil

2 cups (4 oz/125 g) torn spinach leaves

2 sprigs fresh flat-leaf (Italian) parsley

8–10 peppercorns

MAKES ABOUT 2 QT (2 L)

Vegetable Stock

A successful vegetable stock is full flavored, but with no single vegetable dominating the finished product. Making sure that all the vegetables are chopped in uniform shapes and sizes helps them all cook at the same time, and preliminary browning deepens the color, flavor, and body of the stock.

1 Prepare the vegetables

Peel the onions, then chop them into ¼-inch (6-mm) pieces; you should have about 2 cups (8 oz/250 g) chopped onions. Peel the carrots, then cut them into slices ¼ inch thick; you should have about 2 cups (8 oz/250 g) sliced carrots. Brush the mushrooms clean with a soft brush or damp cloth and cut them into pieces the same size as the onions. Cut the leek into slices ¼ inch thick. Seed the bell pepper and chop it into pieces the same size as the onions. (For more details on preparing leeks and peppers turn to pages 33 and 36.) Core and chop the tomatoes into pieces about the same size as the peppers. Cut the celery into slices ¼ inch thick (you should have about 1 cup/5 oz/155 g), then peel and chop the turnip and parsnip into similar-sized pieces. Finally, peel and chop the garlic.

2 Brown the vegetables

Place an 8-qt (8-l) heavy-bottomed pot over medium-high heat. When hot, add the olive oil and heat until the surface appears to shimmer. Add the onions, carrots, mushrooms, leek, and bell pepper and cook, stirring, until the vegetables are golden brown, about 15 minutes. Browning the vegetables before adding the liquid helps to caramelize their natural sugars, thus imparting a deep flavor and golden color to the finished stock.

3 Bring the stock to a boil

Add the spinach, tomatoes, celery, turnip, parsnip, garlic, parsley, and peppercorns to the pot and stir to mix the ingredients. Add water just to cover the ingredients by 1 inch (2.5 cm); more water could dilute the flavor of the stock. Still over medium-high heat and without stirring, slowly bring the liquid to a boil.

Simmer the stock

4 As soon as you see large bubbles begin to form, reduce the heat until only small bubbles occasionally break the surface of the liquid. Keeping the heat at medium to medium-low, simmer, uncovered, until the liquid is reduced by about one-third, 1–1½ hours. Because no collagen is released from the vegetables when making this stock, you don't need to skim the simmering liquid.

Strain the stock

5 Place a fine-mesh sieve over a large tempered-glass or stainless-steel bowl. Ladle or carefully pour the stock through the sieve. Discard the solids that are in the sieve. You can use the stock right away or cool and store it. Because no fat is released from the vegetables when making this stock, you don't need to line the sieve with cheesecloth (muslin).

Cool the stock

6 If you are not using the stock right away, cool it for storage. Fill a large bowl partway with ice water and set the bowl of stock in the ice bath to cool it to room temperature, stirring occasionally.

Store the stock

7 Cover and refrigerate the stock if you plan to use it within 3 days, or ladle or pour it into airtight containers, filling them to within about ½ inch (12 mm) of the rim (the stock expands as it freezes), and freeze for up to 3 months. To thaw frozen stock, refrigerate for 24 hours, or transfer the frozen block of stock to a saucepan and melt slowly over low heat, covered, until liquefied. Then, measure the amount needed for the recipes.

CHEF'S TIP

You can find quantities of quality prepared stocks in the refrigerated case of various high-end grocery stores and specialty-food shops. Cooking with and tasting these stocks is an excellent way to train yourself to recognize what the benchmark of your stock should be.

Fish Stock

You need at least one fish head and a couple of fish frames, or skeletons, all carefully cleaned of any gills, blood, and entrails, to impart the desired light, clean flavor to fish stock. This initial step ensures that the finished stock is perfectly clear, nicely aromatic, and not the least bit "fishy."

4 lb (2 kg) fish head(s) and frames from non-oily fish such as cod, flounder, sea bass, or snapper

¼ cup (2 oz/60 g) plus 1 tablespoon kosher salt

2 sprigs fresh flat-leaf (Italian) parsley

1 sprig fresh thyme

1 bay leaf

½ cup (4 fl oz/125 ml) dry white wine such as Sauvignon Blanc

1 yellow onion, thinly sliced

1 stalk celery, thinly sliced

8–10 peppercorns

MAKES ABOUT 2 QT (2 L)

1 Clean the fish

For the best-flavored stock, it is important that the fish parts be fresh and scrupulously clean. Locate the gills in the side of the head(s) and snip them out with a pair of kitchen scissors. Check the head(s) and frames carefully and pull out any blood vessels or entrails. This is critical, as any blood will make the stock cloudy. Rinse the fish parts thoroughly under running cold water. Break the spine of each frame into 2 or more pieces with the kitchen scissors. Gelatin that will help flavor the stock is in the spine, and this step will encourage its release.

2 Soak the fish

Place the head(s) and frames in a large bowl and add the salt and cool water to cover. Cover and refrigerate for 1 hour. Drain off the salted water, rinse the fish pieces, return them to the bowl, and add clean cool water to cover. Cover and refrigerate again for 1 hour. This two-part soak ensures that the fish pieces are free of blood and impurities.

3 Bring the stock to a boil

Drain the fish pieces, place them in an 8-qt (8-l) heavy-bottomed pot, and add water just to cover by 1 inch (2.5 cm); more water could dilute the flavor of the stock. Place the pot over medium-high heat. Without stirring, slowly bring the liquid to a boil. As soon as you see large bubbles begin to form, reduce the heat until only small bubbles occasionally break the surface of the liquid. Use a large slotted spoon or skimmer to skim the grayish foam that rises to the surface of the liquid. The foam is made up of impurities that are released when the fish parts heat, and it can cloud the finished stock unless it is removed. Continue skimming until the foam no longer forms. Never stir the stock.

Make a bouquet garni

4 Cut a 10-inch (25-cm) square of cheesecloth (muslin); lightly rinse it, and squeeze out the excess water. Have ready an 8-inch (20-cm) length of kitchen string. Put the parsley sprigs, thyme sprig, and bay leaf in the middle of the cheesecloth square, gather the edges together, and tie into a bundle with the string. Enclosing these aromatic ingredients in a cheesecloth bundle helps keep them from interfering with skimming.

Add the aromatic ingredients and simmer the stock

5 When you see that the foam has stopped forming, add the wine, onion, celery, bouquet garni, and peppercorns to the pot. Adjust the heat to maintain a gentle simmer and cook, uncovered, until the liquid has a good fish flavor, about 30 minutes. Do not cook the stock any longer, or it will have an "off" taste.

Strain the stock

6 Cut a piece of cheesecloth large enough to line the inside of a fine-mesh sieve when it is triple layered. Fold the cheesecloth, dampen it with cool water, squeeze it dry, then use it to line the sieve. Place the sieve over a large tempered-glass or stainless-steel bowl. Ladle or carefully pour the stock through the sieve and discard the solids. You can use the stock right away or cool and store it.

Cool and store the stock

7 If you are not using the stock right away, cool it for storage. Fill a large bowl partway with ice water and set the bowl of stock in the ice bath to cool it to room temperature, stirring occasionally. Cover and refrigerate the stock if you plan to use it within 2 days, or ladle or pour it into airtight containers, filling them to within about ½ inch (12 mm) of the rim (the stock expands as it freezes), and freeze for up to 2 months. To thaw frozen stock, refrigerate for 24 hours, or transfer the frozen block of stock to a saucepan and melt slowly over low heat, covered, until liquefied. Then, measure the amount needed for the recipes.

CHEF'S TIP

When making fish stock, always use the bones and heads from firm, white-fleshed, nonoily fish. Parts from oily, fatty fish, such as salmon, mackerel, or tuna, would give the stock an overly strong "fishy" flavor.

Shellfish Stock

The most economical way to make a good shellfish stock is to save the shells from cooked shrimp, lobster, and crab in the freezer until you have accumulated enough. Once you collect about 4 cups (1½ oz/750 g) of shells, you'll be able to make an aromatic stock with a well-rounded flavor and good body.

1 large yellow onion

1 carrot

1 stalk celery

4 cups (1½ lb/750 g) mixed shells from shrimp (prawns), preferably with the heads intact, lobster, or crab

2 sprigs fresh flat-leaf (Italian) parsley

1 sprig fresh thyme

1 bay leaf

½ cup (4 fl oz/125 ml) dry white wine such as Sauvignon Blanc

2 tablespoons tomato paste

8–10 peppercorns

1 tablespoon kosher salt

MAKES ABOUT 2 QT (2 L)

1 Cut the vegetables

Cut the onion in half lengthwise and peel each half. Place the onion halves, cut side down, on the cutting board. Cut each half crosswise into thick slices. Next, peel the carrot, then cut it on the diagonal into ½-inch (12-mm) pieces. Finally, cut the celery into the same-sized pieces as the carrot.

2 Prepare the shells

Using a large, heavy knife, chop the shrimp shells into small pieces. Don't chop the shells too finely or they will be harder to strain. Put the lobster or crab shells, if using, in a heavy-duty locking plastic bag and, using a rolling pin or a meat pounder, break the shells into small pieces.

3 Bring the stock to a boil

Place all the shells in an 8-qt (8-l) heavy-bottomed pot. Add water just to cover the shells by 1 inch (2.5 cm); more water could dilute the flavor of the stock. Place the pot over medium-high heat. Without stirring, slowly bring the liquid to a boil. As soon as you see large bubbles begin to form, reduce the heat so that only small bubbles occasionally break the surface of the liquid. Use a large slotted spoon or a skimmer to skim the grayish foam that rises to the surface of the liquid. The foam is made up of impurities that are released when the shells heat, and it can cloud the finished stock unless it is removed. Continue skimming until the foam no longer forms. Never stir the stock.

4 Make a bouquet garni

Cut a 10-inch (25-cm) square of cheesecloth (muslin); lightly rinse it, and squeeze out the excess water. Have ready an 8-inch (20-cm) length of kitchen string. Put the parsley sprigs, thyme sprig, and bay leaf in the middle of the cheesecloth square, gather the edges together, and tie into a bundle with the string. Enclosing these aromatic ingredients in a cheesecloth bundle helps keep them from interfering with skimming.

5 Add the vegetables and flavorings and simmer the stock

When you see that the foam has stopped forming, add the wine, onion, carrot, celery, tomato paste, bouquet garni, and peppercorns. Adjust the heat to maintain a gentle simmer and cook, uncovered, until the liquid has a good shellfish flavor, about 30 minutes. Stir in the salt and remove the pot from the heat.

6 Strain the stock

Cut a piece of cheesecloth (muslin) large enough to line the inside of a fine-mesh sieve when it is triple layered. Fold the cheesecloth, dampen it with cool water, squeeze it dry, then use it to line the sieve. Place the sieve over a large tempered-glass or stainless-steel bowl. Ladle or carefully pour the stock through the sieve. Discard the solids that are in the sieve. You can use the stock right away or cool and store it.

7 Cool and store the stock

If you are not using the stock right away, cool it for storage. Fill a large bowl partway with ice water and set the bowl of stock in the ice bath to cool it to room temperature, stirring occasionally. Cover and refrigerate the stock if you plan to use it within 2 days, or ladle or pour it into airtight containers, filling them to within about ½ inch (12 mm) of the rim (the stock expands as it freezes), and freeze for up to 2 months. To thaw frozen stock, refrigerate for 24 hours, or transfer the frozen block of stock to a saucepan and melt slowly over low heat, covered, until liquefied. Then, measure the amount needed for the recipes.

CHEF'S TIP

Keep in mind that some people might like more or less salt in their soups than you will. It is a good idea to take that into account when preparing stocks, soups, and stews and not add too much salt at the beginning of cooking a dish. Remember, you can always put more salt into a soup or stew, but you can't take out an excess of salt.

2

Key Techniques

Mastering a handful of basic kitchen skills will help you prepare a wide array of soups and stews. In this chapter, you will learn invaluable techniques, from how to purée a soup base to how to clean shellfish. Each technique is explained in clear step-by-step text and photographs. If you encounter a technique you aren't sure about in a recipe, you can always turn to this chapter for help.

Dicing an Onion

TECHNIQUE

1 Cut the onion in half

Using a chef's knife, cut the onion in half lengthwise, through the root end. This makes it easier to peel and gives each half a flat side for stability when making your cuts.

2 Peel the onion

Using a paring knife, pick up the edge of the onion's papery skin at the stem end and pull it away. You may also need to remove the first layer of onion if it, too, has rough or papery patches.

3 Trim the onion

Trim each end neatly, leaving some of the root intact to help hold the onion half together. Place an onion half, flat side down, on the cutting board with the root end facing away from you.

4 Cut the onion lengthwise

Hold the onion securely on either side. Using a chef's knife, make a series of lengthwise cuts as thick as you want the final dice to be. Do not cut all the way through the root end.

5 Cut the onion horizontally

Spread your fingers across the onion to help keep it together. Turn the knife blade parallel to the cutting board and make a series of horizontal cuts as thick as you want the final dice to be.

6 Dice the onion

Still holding the onion together with your fingers, cut it crosswise to make dice. Dicing an onion in this methodical way gives you pieces that cook evenly.

Working with Leeks

1 Trim the leeks
Using a chef's knife, trim off the roots and dark green tops of the leeks, leaving only the white and pale green parts. If the outer layer is wilted or discolored, peel away and discard.

2 Halve and quarter the leeks
Cut each leek in half lengthwise. Place each half, cut side down, and halve it again to create quarters.

Mincing Garlic

1 Peel the garlic clove
Place the garlic clove on a work surface. Using the flat side of a chef's knife, press against the clove. The papery skin will split, making the clove easier to peel.

3 Rinse the leeks
Separating the layers with your fingers to expose any sand or dirt, swish the leeks in a bowl of water. You can also rinse the leeks under running water while separating the layers.

4 Slice the leeks crosswise
Holding the layers of each quarter together, pat the leeks dry with a kitchen towel. Using a chef's knife, cut the leek quarters crosswise into slices.

2 Mince the garlic
Cut the garlic into very thin slices, then gather the slices together on the board. Rock the knife rhythmically over the slices until they are cut into very fine pieces.

Dicing Carrots

1 Trim the carrots

Start with good-quality, unblemished carrots. Use a vegetable peeler to remove the rough skin. Switch to a chef's knife and trim off the leafy tops and rootlike ends.

2 Cut the carrots into lengths

Cut the carrots into even lengths no longer than about 3 inches (7.5 cm). Shorter pieces are simpler to handle, making cutting and then dicing easier.

3 Create a flat surface

Before cutting each length of carrot, cut a thin slice from one side to create a flat surface. Turn the carrot piece onto this flat side to keep it stable while you cut.

4 Cut the lengths into slices

Cut the carrot piece lengthwise into slices as thick as you want the final dice to be. (For example, if you are aiming for ¼-inch/6-mm dice, cut the carrot into ¼-inch slices.)

5 Cut the slices into sticks

Stack 2 or 3 carrot slices and turn them so they are lying on their wide sides. Cut them lengthwise into sticks that are as thick as the first slices.

6 Cut the sticks into dice

Cut the carrot sticks crosswise to create dice. Dicing carrots methodically creates evenly sized pieces that cook at the same rate. Repeat with the remaining carrot lengths.

Dicing Celery

1 Trim the root end

Start with firm, unblemished celery with fresh-looking leaves. Using a chef's knife, trim the head of the celery as needed where the stalks meet the root end. Rinse the stalks.

2 Chop the leaves (optional)

The leaves are used in some dishes to provide extra celery flavor. Cut the leaves from the stalks and chop as directed in a recipe, usually coarsely.

TROUBLESHOOTING

Some celery today is string free, but you may still encounter stringy stalks. The outside ribs may have a tough outer layer as well. To remove this layer or any strings, run a vegetable peeler over the stalk.

3 Cut the celery into lengths

Cut the celery stalks into even lengths no longer than about 3 inches (7.5 cm). Shorter pieces are simpler to handle, making slicing and then dicing easier.

4 Cut the lengths into sticks

Cut the celery pieces lengthwise into sticks as thick as you want the final dice to be. (For example, if you are aiming for ¼-inch/6-mm dice, cut the celery into ¼-inch-thick sticks.)

5 Cut the sticks into dice

Cut the celery sticks crosswise to create dice. Dicing celery methodically creates evenly sized pieces that cook at the same rate. Repeat with the remaining celery lengths.

Working with Peppers & Chiles

1 Halve the pepper

Using a chef's knife, cut the pepper (capsicum) in half lengthwise. If cutting chiles, wear latex gloves.

Peeling Plum Tomatoes

1 Score the tomatoes

Use a paring knife to cut a small, shallow X in the blossom end, or bottom, of each plum (Roma) tomato. This process, known as *scoring*, will help you remove the skin quickly later.

2 Blanch the tomatoes

Bring a pot of water to a boil. Using a slotted spoon, plunge the tomatoes in the boiling water for 15–30 seconds, or until the skins are just loosened. This brief cooking is called *blanching*.

2 Clean the pepper

Use your fingers or a small knife to remove the stem, seeds, and ribs, or membranes. Then, cut the pepper or chile as directed in the recipe.

3 Shock the tomatoes

Use the slotted spoon to transfer the blanched tomatoes to a bowl of ice water. This process is known as *shocking*, and it will stop the tomatoes from cooking too much.

4 Peel off the tomato skins

As soon as the tomatoes are cool, remove them from the ice water. Use a paring knife to pull off the skin, starting at the X. The skin should now peel off quickly and easily.

Seeding & Dicing Plum Tomatoes

1 Cut the tomato in half
Plum (roma) tomatoes are a good choice for using in soups, as they have a high flesh-to-seed ratio. Use a chef's knife to cut peeled tomatoes in half lengthwise.

2 Squeeze and scoop out the seeds
Gently squeeze the tomato half over a bowl. Use a fingertip, if needed, to help scoop out the seed sacs and watery pulp.

TROUBLESHOOTING
After removing the seeds, you may see white or yellow patches that were not evident when the tomato was whole. These spots indicate poor flavor and texture; trim them away or discard the tomato.

3 Remove the stem
Use a paring knife to make a V-shaped cut in the top of each tomato half to remove the green stem. Take care not to remove too much of the tomato flesh when you cut.

4 Cut lengthwise slices
Place one of the tomato halves cut side down. Using a chef's knife, make a series of lengthwise cuts, about ¼ inch (6 mm) apart.

5 Cut the strips into dice
Line up the strips and cut them crosswise into ¼-inch dice. Push the dice aside to keep them separate from your work area. Repeat steps 3–5 with the remaining tomatoes.

Peeling & Deveining Shrimp

1 Pull off the head and legs

Work with one shrimp (prawn) at a time, keeping the others in a bowl filled with ice. Pull off the head, if it is still attached, and then the legs on the inside curve of the shell.

2 Pull the shell from the meat

Starting at the head end, carefully pull away the shell from the meat. You can reserve and freeze the shells for stock.

3 Make a shallow groove

Using a paring knife, make a shallow cut down the back of each shrimp. You will see the dark, veinlike, intestinal tract running through the meat.

4 Remove the vein

With the tip of the knife, lift out and pull away the dark vein, gently scraping it if necessary. The vein, while not harmful, is neither attractive nor palatable to most people.

5 Rinse the shrimp

Place the peeled and deveined shrimp in a colander and rinse them with cold water to remove any residual grit left from the vein.

TROUBLESHOOTING

Choose firm, sweet-smelling shrimp still in the shell, if possible. Avoid shrimp with any visible yellowing. Unless you are buying spotted shrimp, be sure to avoid shrimp that show signs of speckling.

TECHNIQUE

Cleaning Clams & Mussels

1 Soak the clams and mussels
Place the clams or mussels in a bowl of salt water for 10 minutes to purge any sand caught in the shells. Dissolve 6 tablespoons (3 oz/90 g) of salt per 4 qt (4 l) of tap water.

2 Scrub the shells
If the mussel or clam shells still feel gritty after the initial soaking, using a stiff-bristled brush, scrub them well under running water.

3 Or, wipe the shells
If the mussel or clam shells do not feel gritty after the initial soaking, use a damp kitchen towel to wipe all of the shells clean.

4 Debeard the mussels
Remove the beard (the little fibrous tufts the mussel uses to connect to rocks or pilings) from each mussel by cutting or scraping it with a paring knife or kitchen scissors.

5 Rinse the clams and mussels
Gently place the clams or mussels in a colander and give them a final rinsing before using them in the recipe. If you are not cooking them right away, keep the shellfish in the refrigerator.

TROUBLESHOOTING
Carefully examine each clam or mussel for cracked or broken shells; this is a sign that the mollusk is dead and must be discarded. Also discard any mollusk that does not close to the touch.

Making a Roux

1 Combine the butter and flour

Melt the butter in a heavy-bottomed pan. Wait until the butter stops foaming before sprinkling in the flour. Whisk together over low heat to combine and to prevent lumping.

2 Make a white roux

For a white roux, cook the butter and flour over low heat for 2–3 minutes, stirring constantly. The roux should be a pale straw color and have a lightly toasted taste.

Thickening with a Roux

1 Add the hot liquid

Gradually add the hot liquid to the roux while whisking to ensure the liquid and roux are fully combined.

3 Make a brown roux

For a brown roux, cook the butter and flour over medium heat for about 20 minutes, stirring constantly. The roux will be a deep, reddish brown and have a nutty taste.

TROUBLESHOOTING

Adjust the heat and keep a close watch on the heat level of the burner. You want the roux to bubble very gently. If the roux cooks too quickly, it will burn and become gritty.

2 Adjust the consistency

Soups thickened with a roux have an opaque appearance. If the mixture becomes too thick, thin it with a little more of the hot liquid used in the soup recipe.

Mincing Herbs

1 Separate the leaves

Using your fingers, pluck the leaves from the herb sprigs and discard the stems. Gather the leaves together into a pile on the cutting board. Shown here is flat-leaf (Italian) parsley.

2 Mince the herbs

Rest your fingertips on the knife tip and rock the knife over the board to cut the leaves into coarse pieces (chopped) or fine pieces (minced). Stop occasionally to clean the knife.

Browning Meat

1 Season the meat

Pat the pieces dry with paper towels; this helps prevent steaming and ensures a crisp exterior. Spread the pieces out on a baking sheet. Season, turning the pieces to coat evenly.

2 Add the meat to the pan

In a large, heavy frying pan over medium heat, warm the olive oil until hot enough to sizzle a piece of meat on contact. Add the meat, a small handful at a time.

3 Brown the meat

Use tongs to turn the pieces of meat to ensure even color. Browning meat caramelizes the surface, which results in a rich flavor and attractive and appetizing appearance.

TROUBLESHOOTING

A crowded pan such as this will cause the meat to steam instead of brown. To prevent this from happening, brown the meat in batches, removing each batch as it is ready.

Puréeing Soups with a Food Processor

1 Add the soup to the work bowl

Working in batches, ladle a small amount of the soup into the work bowl of a food processor, taking care not to overfill the bowl. Working in batches ensures an even consistency.

2 Process the soup

Secure the top on the food processor and pulse the soup a few time to combine the liquid and solids slightly. Then turn on the motor and process the soup until it is smooth.

Puréeing Soups with a Blender

1 Add the soup to the blender

Working in batches, ladle soup into the blender, filling it 2 inches (5 cm) short of the top.

3 Scrape down the sides

During processing, stop the machine a few times and use a rubber spatula to scrape down the sides of the work bowl. This scraping helps guarantee an even consistency.

TROUBLESHOOTING

If the soup begins to ooze from the bottom of the food processor, you have filled the bowl too full. Stop the machine and remove some of the soup mixture. Then, continue to process the soup as directed.

2 Process the soup

Start blending on low speed, then gradually increase it. Keep your hand, protected with a towel or oven mitt, on the top of the blender; the steam from hot liquids can force the lid off.

Puréeing Soups with a Food Mill

1 Fit the disk into the food mill

Fit the food mill with a grinding disk: For a rustic texture, use the larger-holed disk; for a smooth texture, use the smaller-holed disk. Use the medium disk for a texture in between.

2 Secure the food mill over a bowl

Secure the crank mechanism according to the manufacturer's directions, then fit the food mill securely over a large bowl. Ladle the soup into the food mill.

Puréeing with an Immersion Blender

1 Insert the wand into the soup

Push the blender's wand into the soup. Be sure that the blade is completely submerged to prevent spattering.

3 Process the soup

Holding the handle securely with one hand, slowly turn the crank of the food mill. This action purées the soup solids and helps to extract as much flavor from them as possible.

4 Scrape the food mill

After processing, use a rubber spatula to scrape any puréed soup off the bottom of the food mill. Discard the solids inside the mill.

2 Process the soup

Turn on the blender and move the wand around the soup to make sure you achieve an even texture. When finished, wait until the blade stops spinning before removing.

3

Clear Soups

Each soup in this chapter is built on a clear, full-bodied, richly flavored stock—the perfect beginning. Aromatic vegetables, tender chicken meat, or briny clams are added to it to create such favorites as a chunky minestrone, a homey chicken soup, or a hearty chowder. As you work your way through the recipes, you will learn new skills that will come in handy for making countless other soups.

Chicken Soup

A good chicken soup holds the promise of garden-fresh vegetables and bite-sized chicken pieces simmered in a rich, clear, full-bodied stock. Using a time-honored technique, here the whole chicken is brined before making the soup to ensure that the meat is juicy and flavorful and the stock is doubly rich.

1 Combine the stock ingredients
If you need help making chicken stock, turn to page 18. In an 8-qt (8-l) heavy-bottomed pot, combine the chicken parts, onion, carrot, celery, garlic, parsley, bay leaf, and peppercorns. Add water just to cover the ingredients by 1 inch (2.5 cm).

2 Bring the stock to a boil
Place the pot over medium-high heat. Without stirring, slowly bring the liquid to a boil. As soon as you see large bubbles begin to form, reduce the heat until only small bubbles occasionally break the surface of the liquid. Use a large spoon to skim the grayish foam that rises to the surface as the liquid reaches a boil, then continue skimming, without stirring, for the first 10 minutes.

3 Simmer the stock
Simmer the stock, uncovered, adjusting the heat periodically to keep the stock at a slow simmer, for 2–2½ hours, adding more water, if necessary, to keep the ingredients just covered. Do not stir, but continue to skim the surface as needed, usually every 30 minutes or so.

4 Strain the stock
Line a fine-mesh sieve with a triple layer of cheesecloth (muslin) that has been dampened and squeezed dry, and place it over a large bowl. Place the bowl in the sink, if you like, to make cleanup easier. Using a slotted spoon, remove the larger solids, then ladle or carefully pour the stock through the sieve. Discard the solids in the sieve.

5 Cool and defat the stock
If you are using the stock immediately, use a large spoon to skim and discard the fat from the surface of the stock, measure out 3 qt (3 l), and proceed to step 6. If you are not using the stock right away, cool it in an ice bath until it is at least room temperature. Cover the stock and refrigerate it overnight. The next day, use a large spoon to lift off the fat solidified on the top. Measure out 3 qt (3 l) of the stock and set it aside for the soup. Cover and refrigerate the remaining stock for up to 3 days or freeze for up to 3 months.

For the chicken stock

6 lb (3 kg) chicken necks and backs

1 large or 2 medium yellow onions, quartered through the stem end

1 large carrot, peeled and cut into 1-inch (2.5-cm) lengths

1 large stalk celery with leaves, cut into 1-inch (2.5-cm) lengths

1 clove garlic, peeled

3 or 4 sprigs fresh flat-leaf (Italian) parsley

1 bay leaf

8–10 whole peppercorns

1 chicken, about 3½ lb (1.75 kg), giblets removed if present

¼ cup (2 oz/60 g) kosher salt, plus ½ teaspoon

2 stalks celery

1 yellow onion

2 carrots

⅛ teaspoon freshly ground pepper

Chopped fresh flat-leaf (Italian) parsley for garnish, optional

MAKES 4–6 SERVINGS

SHORTCUT

If you do not have time to make your own chicken stock, use 3 qt (3 l) prepared chicken stock and begin the recipe with step 6.

6

7

Briefly brining the whole chicken in salt water before cooking it in the stock tenderizes the meat and improves the overall flavor of the bird and soup.

An excess of foam rises to the surface of stock as the chicken simmers. This foam is mostly composed of collagen and gelatin from the chicken and should be skimmed with a large metal spoon to ensure a clear, flavorful soup.

6 Brine the chicken

Do not remove any skin or fat from the chicken; they will help to flavor the soup. Choose a bowl that is large enough to hold the chicken with 2 inches (5 cm) to spare at the top. Place the chicken in the bowl and add cold water to cover. Drain and repeat a second time. Return the chicken to the empty bowl, sprinkle the ¼ cup salt evenly over it, and then again add cold water to cover by at least 1 inch (2.5 cm). Let the chicken stand in the salt water for about 30 minutes. Refrigerate the chicken during this time if the kitchen is warm. I have discovered that this brief brining in salted water ensures that the cooked chicken meat will be juicy and tender.

7 Add the stock to the chicken

Cooking a whole chicken in chicken stock makes a rich, double-chicken flavor perfect for a satisfying bowl of soup. Drain the chicken from its brine and place it in a large, heavy-bottomed pot. Add the reserved stock. Place the pot over medium-high heat. Without stirring, slowly bring the liquid to a boil. As soon as you see large bubbles begin to form, reduce the heat until only small bubbles occasionally break the surface of the liquid.

8 Cook the chicken in the stock

Use a large spoon to skim any grayish foam that rises to the surface of the liquid, then continue skimming, without stirring, for the first 10 minutes. Simmer the stock, uncovered, adjusting the heat periodically to keep the stock at a slow simmer, until a leg starts to separate from the body of the chicken when pulled or prodded with tongs or a large spoon, about 1½ hours. Do not stir, but continue to skim the surface every 30 minutes or so.

9 Prepare the vegetables

While the soup is simmering, cut all the vegetables so that they are ready to go into the pot. If you're not sure how to dice celery, onions, and carrots, turn to pages 35, 32, and 34. First, dice the celery: Trim the ends of the celery stalks and cut them into ¼-inch (6-mm) dice. Next, dice the onion: Cut the onion in half lengthwise and peel each half. One at a time, place the onion halves, cut side down, on the cutting board. Make a series of lengthwise cuts perpendicular to the board, then a series of horizontal cuts with the knife blade parallel to the cutting board, and lastly cut crosswise to create ¼-inch dice. Be sure to stop just short of the root end; it holds the onion together as you cut. Finally, dice the carrots: Peel the carrots, then cut them into ¼-inch (6-mm) dice. Remember, it's more important to yield uniformly sized pieces than perfect cuts. The more you practice, the more skilled you will become at using a knife.

10 Remove the chicken from the pot

Remove the pot from the heat. Using a large spoon, carefully break the cooked chicken into sections while it is still in the pot. Using tongs or a slotted spoon, transfer the chicken pieces to a large, deep platter and let the chicken pieces stand until they are cool enough to handle, about 20 minutes.

11 Defat the soup

Using a large metal spoon, carefully skim and discard the fat from the surface of the soup. This process may take a while, but it is important to remove as much fat as possible to ensure a clean-tasting, full-flavored soup.

12 Shred the chicken

When the chicken is cool enough to handle, pull off the skin and discard it. (Some of the skin may have fallen off into the soup; be sure to remove it.) Use a knife to cut away the breast, leg, and thigh meat from the bone. Shred the meat into spoon-sized pieces to yield 1½ cups (9 oz/280 g) of shredded chicken meat. Reserve the remaining meat for another use.

13 Add the vegetables and shredded chicken to the soup

Preheat the oven to 200°F (95°C) and place individual bowls in the oven to warm. Add the carrots, celery, onion, and the ½ teaspoon salt to the soup, place over medium heat, and bring to a simmer. Cover and cook for 5 minutes. Uncover, adjust the heat to low so that the soup is at a gentle simmer, and stir the soup once or twice. Cook for 5 minutes, then add the shredded chicken. Continue to cook until all the vegetables are tender and the chicken is heated through, about 5 minutes longer.

14 Adjust the seasonings

Add the pepper and mix well. Taste the soup. If you feel it tastes bland, add more salt and pepper a little at a time, stirring, and tasting after each addition until the seasonings are to your liking.

15 Serve the soup

Ladle the soup into the warmed bowls, garnish with the parsley, if using, and serve right away.

CHEF'S TIP

If you have a degreasing cup, you can use it to remove the fat from the soup's surface, instead of skimming with a spoon. Working in batches, ladle the soup into a large degreasing cup. The soup will settle to the bottom, where it can be easily poured off through the long spout, leaving the fat behind.

Finishing touches

A bowl of homemade hearty chicken soup is already layered with rich flavors, but a special touch, added at the end, can make the soup even more delicious. A fine dice of parsley and lemon zest brightens both the color and flavor of your soup, while julienned green onion adds an Asian accent. Parmesan cheese crisps are easy to make and wonderfully crunchy when eaten on the side or crumbled into the bowl.

Fresh herbs and lemon zest (top left)
Mix together 2 teaspoons grated lemon zest and 2 tablespoons minced fresh flat-leaf (Italian) parsley and sprinkle on the soup just before serving.

Parmesan cheese crisps (left)
Coat a baking sheet with nonstick cooking spray. Grate 1½ cups (6 oz/185 g) Parmigiano-Reggiano cheese. Form 1-tablespoon piles of cheese evenly spaced on the sheet. Bake in a preheated 350°F (180°C) oven until golden, about 5 minutes.

Julienned green onion (above)
Thinly slice a green (spring) onion lengthwise into 1-inch (2.5-cm) strips about ¼ inch (6 mm) wide. Place the strips in ice water until they curl.

Chicken Soup Variations

Once you have mastered basic Chicken Soup (page 47), you will have learned how to make a rich stock, including how to skim and defat it for clarity; how to brine a whole chicken; and how to chop and slice a variety of common soup vegetables, including carrots, celery, and onions. Armed with these new skills, you can now transform this classic soup into half a dozen new soups by changing only a few ingredients. Some of these are classics, such as Matzoh Ball Soup and Chicken Noodle Soup, while others reflect an ethnic pantry, including Chicken with Egg Threads & Parmesan, Tortilla Soup, and Asian Chicken Soup. Each variation makes 4 to 6 servings.

Chicken Noodle Soup

The addition of noodles results in a hearty soup that is suitable for serving as a main course.

Follow the recipe to make Chicken Soup. In step 13, add ¼ lb (125 g) wide egg noodles, broken into 1–2-inch (2.5–5-cm) lengths, along with the vegetables and salt.

Cook until the vegetables and noodles are tender and the chicken is heated through, about 8 minutes longer.

Proceed with the recipe to adjust the seasonings and serve the soup.

Chicken & Rice Soup with Escarole

Escarole is a slightly bitter and versatile green that complements nearly any chicken soup. The rice gives the soup added body.

Brine one 3½-lb (1.75-kg) chicken with ¼ cup (2 oz/60 g) kosher salt. Drain, then cook the chicken in 1 batch Chicken Stock (page 18) for about 1½ hours. Remove the chicken from the pot, defat the soup, and shred the chicken. Measure out 1½ cups (9 oz/280 g) shredded meat; reserve the remainder for another use.

Add ½ cup (3½ oz/105 g) long-grain white rice to the soup, cover partially, and cook over low heat until the rice is almost tender, about 15 minutes. Add 2 cups (6 oz/185 g) torn escarole leaves, 2 peeled and diced carrots, 1 diced yellow onion, and the chicken meat. Cover and cook until the vegetables and rice are fully tender and the chicken is heated through, about 5 minutes.

Adjust the seasonings and serve right away garnished with ¼ cup (1 oz/30 g) freshly grated Parmigiano-Reggiano cheese.

Chicken Soup with Egg Threads & Parmesan

Beaten eggs, English peas, and Parmigiano-Reggiano cheese turn a simple chicken soup into the classic Italian *stracciatella*.

Brine one 3½-lb (1.75-kg) chicken with ¼ cup (2 oz/60 g) kosher salt. Drain, then cook the chicken in 1 batch Chicken Stock (page 18) for about 1½ hours. Remove the chicken from the pot, defat the soup, and shred the chicken. Measure out 1½ cups (9 oz/280 g) shredded meat; reserve the remainder for another use.

Add 1 cup (5 oz/155 g) fresh shelled English peas (1 lb/500 g unshelled) or frozen petite peas to the soup, raise the heat to medium-high, and bring to a gentle boil. In a small bowl, beat 3 large eggs and ⅓ cup (3 fl oz/80 ml) water until frothy. In a slow, steady stream, add the egg mixture to the soup while stirring constantly and slowly with a slotted spoon. The eggs will set, forming short threads. Reduce the heat to low and stir in the chicken meat and ½ cup (2 oz/60 g) grated Parmigiano-Reggiano cheese. Simmer until heated through, about 5 minutes. Adjust the seasonings and serve right away.

Matzoh Ball Soup

There are thousands of "authentic" recipes for matzoh ball soup. Here, the matzoh balls are cooked in the intensely flavored chicken stock and then combined with shredded chicken.

In a bowl, whisk together 2 large eggs, 2 tablespoons vegetable oil, 2 tablespoons water, and ½ teaspoon kosher salt. Sprinkle ½ cup (2 oz/60 g) matzoh meal and ¼ teaspoon baking powder over the egg mixture and gently mix with a rubber spatula just until combined. Cover and refrigerate for 2 hours.

Meanwhile, brine one 3½-lb (1.75-kg) chicken with ¼ cup (2 oz/60 g) kosher salt. Drain, then cook the chicken in 1 batch Chicken Stock (page 18) for about 1½ hours. Remove the chicken from the pot, defat the soup, and shred the chicken. Measure out 8 cups (64 fl oz/2 l) of the stock and 1½ cups (9 oz/280 g) shredded meat; reserve the remainder for another use.

Form the chilled matzoh mixture into twelve 1-inch (2.5-cm) balls, handling them as little as possible. Pour the stock into a saucepan large enough to hold the matzoh balls in a single layer and bring to a boil. Gently place the matzoh balls in the boiling stock, reduce the heat to low, and simmer, uncovered, until the balls are light and fluffy, 20–25 minutes. Adjust the seasonings.

With a slotted spoon, evenly divide the matzoh balls and shredded chicken among 6 bowls. Ladle in the hot stock and garnish with 2 tablespoons minced fresh dill, dividing evenly. Serve right away.

Tortilla Soup

Lime juice, avocado, and green onions lend a Mexican flavor to this version.

Brine one 3½-lb (1.75-kg) chicken with ¼ cup (2 oz/60 g) kosher salt. Drain, then cook the chicken in 1 batch Chicken Stock (page 18) for about 1½ hours. Remove the chicken from the pot, defat the soup, and shred the chicken. Measure out 8 cups (64 fl oz/2 l) of the stock and 1½ cups (9 oz/280 g) shredded meat; reserve the remainder for another use.

Pour the stock into a large saucepan and bring to a boil. Add 1 diced tomato, 1 minced large jalapeño chile, 1 minced garlic clove, 1 teaspoon kosher salt, and the shredded chicken. Reduce the heat to low and simmer until heated through, about 5 minutes. Stir in 2 tablespoons fresh lime juice. Adjust the seasonings.

Divide 1 peeled and diced avocado and 4 thinly sliced green (spring) onions (white and tender green parts), evenly among 4 bowls. Ladle in the hot stock and garnish with 3 cups (24 oz/750 g) broken corn tortilla chips and 2 tablespoons minced fresh cilantro (fresh coriander), dividing evenly. Serve right away.

Asian Chicken Soup

The addition of snow peas, sesame oil, soy sauce, and ginger gives traditional chicken soup an Asian flavor.

Brine one 3½-lb (1.75-kg) chicken with ¼ cup (2 oz/60 g) kosher salt. Drain, then cook the chicken in 1 batch Chicken Stock (page 18) for about 1½ hours. Remove the chicken from the pot, defat the soup, and shred the chicken. Measure out 8 cups (64 fl oz/2 l) of the stock and 1½ cups (9 oz/280 g) shredded meat; reserve the remainder for another use.

Pour the stock into a large saucepan and bring to a boil. Add 2 cups (6 oz/185 g) thinly sliced fresh cremini or shiitake mushroom caps; ½ cup (2½ oz/75 g) snow pea (mangetout) pieces (⅜-inch/1-cm pieces); 1 tablespoon peeled and minced fresh ginger; 4 slivered green (spring) onions (white and tender green parts), 2 tablespoons soy sauce; 1 teaspoon kosher salt, and the shredded chicken. Reduce the heat to low and simmer until heated through, about 5 minutes. Stir in 1 teaspoon Asian sesame oil and ⅛ teaspoon white pepper. Adjust the seasonings and serve right away.

French Onion Soup

The secret to a rich-flavored and deeply colored onion soup is the small amount of sugar added to the slowly cooking onions. It supplements the vegetable's naturally occurring sugar, which helps the onions to caramelize as they cook. A crown of bread and melted cheese further enriches the finished soup.

1 Brown the meats and vegetables for the stock

If you need help making Brown Beef Stock, turn to page 22. Position a rack in the upper third of the oven and preheat to 400°F (200°C). Lightly oil a large roasting pan. Spread the marrowbones, beef shin, carrots, celery, and onion in the pan. Roast, turning the meats and vegetables once or twice, until all the ingredients are a deep mahogany brown, about 45 minutes. Using tongs, transfer the meat and the vegetables to an 8-qt (8-l) heavy-bottomed pot.

2 Deglaze the roasting pan

Protecting your hand with an oven mitt, tip the roasting pan and use a spoon to remove the clear fat that collects in the corner. Place the roasting pan over 2 burners, turn on the heat to low, and add the water. Using a wide wooden spatula, scrape up the browned bits from the pan bottom and stir to dissolve them in the water. They will add a deep caramelized flavor and rich amber color to the finished stock.

3 Bring the stock to a boil, then simmer

Pour the contents of the roasting pan into the pot holding the browned ingredients. Add the parsley, bay leaf, and peppercorns. Add water just to cover the ingredients by 1 inch (2.5 cm). Without stirring, slowly bring the liquid to a boil over medium-high heat. As soon as you see large bubbles begin to form, reduce the heat until only small bubbles occasionally break the surface of the liquid. Use a large slotted spoon or skimmer to skim the grayish foam that rises to the surface of the liquid for the first 10 minutes of cooking. Never stir the stock, which will make it cloudy. Simmer the stock, uncovered, adjusting the heat periodically to keep the stock at a gentle simmer, for 3–4 hours. Continue to skim the surface every 30 minutes or so. Add more water if necessary to keep the ingredients covered.

4 Strain the stock

Line a fine-mesh sieve with a triple layer of cheesecloth (muslin) that has been dampened and squeezed dry, and place the sieve over a large tempered-glass or stainless-steel bowl. Place the bowl in the sink, if you like, to make cleanup easier. Using a slotted spoon, remove the larger solids, then ladle or carefully pour the stock through the sieve. Discard the solids that are in the sieve.

For the brown beef stock

Canola oil for preparing the pan

3 lb (1.5 kg) beef marrowbones, cracked by the butcher

2 thick slices meaty beef shin, about 2 lb (1 kg) total weight

2 large carrots, peeled and cut on the diagonal into ½-inch (12-mm) pieces

2 stalks celery with leaves, cut on the diagonal into ½-inch (12-mm) pieces

1 large yellow onion, cut into 1-inch (2.5-cm) cubes

2 cups (16 fl oz/500 ml) water for deglazing

3 or 4 sprigs fresh flat-leaf (Italian) parsley

1 bay leaf

8–10 whole peppercorns

2½ lb (1.25 kg) yellow onions

2 tablespoons unsalted butter

1 tablespoon canola oil

1 teaspoon sugar

½ cup (4 fl oz/125 ml) dry white wine such as Sauvignon Blanc

1½ teaspoons kosher salt

⅛ teaspoon freshly ground pepper

8 round slices Italian or French bread, each ½ inch (12 mm) thick

Wedge of Gruyère cheese (at least 2 oz/60 g)

MAKES 4 SERVINGS

6

5 Defat the stock

If you are using the stock immediately, use a large spoon to skim and discard the fat from the surface of the stock, measure out 6 cups (48 fl oz/1.5 l), and proceed to step 6. If you are not using the stock right away, cool it in an ice bath until it is at least room temperature. Cover the stock and refrigerate it overnight. The next day, use a large spoon to lift off the fat solidified on the top. Measure out 6 cups (48 fl oz/1.5 l) of the stock and set it aside for the soup. Cover and refrigerate the remaining stock for up to 3 days or freeze for up to 3 months.

6 Prepare the onions

Cut each onion in half lengthwise and peel each half. One at a time, place the onion halves, cut side down, on a cutting board, and thinly slice them lengthwise.

7 Caramelize the onions

Place a large, heavy-bottomed pot over medium-low heat and add the butter and oil. When the butter has melted and the foam begins to subside, add the onions and stir them with a wooden spoon, coating them evenly with the fat. Reduce the heat to low, cover, and cook, stirring occasionally and adjusting the heat as necessary if the onions are cooking too quickly, for 15 minutes. Uncover the pan, sprinkle the onions with the sugar, and stir thoroughly to blend. The sugar augments the naturally occurring sugar in the onions, which helps the browning process. Now, continue cooking uncovered, stirring often, until the onions are a rich golden brown, about 25 minutes longer. When the onions cook at this slow pace the sugars caramelize, causing the flavors of the onions to intensify and become more complex.

8 Deglaze the pot

Add the wine to the pot and raise the heat to high, scraping the bottom of the pot with the wooden spoon to loosen any browned bits. Bring to a boil and continue scraping to ensure that all the flavor is incorporated.

SHORTCUT

If you do not have time to make your own brown beef stock, use 6 cups (48 fl oz/1.5 l) prepared brown beef stock and begin the recipe with step 6.

9 Simmer the soup

Add the reserved 6 cups stock, the salt, and the pepper to the pot and return to a boil. As soon as you see large bubbles begin to form, adjust the heat so that the soup simmers gently. Cover the pot and cook until the onions are tender but still hold their shape and the broth has a rich onion-beef flavor, about 30 minutes. Check every now and again to make sure the soup is not cooking too quickly, which can cause the onions to break down too much and become mushy.

CHEF'S TIP

Although storing your onions in a cool, dark, dry place is preferable to keeping them in the refrigerator, chilling them for a few hours before cooking is the best way to help prevent your eyes from tearing when you cut, slice, or dice them.

10 Toast the bread and shred the cheese

Meanwhile, preheat the oven to 450°F (230°C). Arrange the bread slices on a baking sheet, place in the oven, and toast until golden brown on the bottom side, about 5 minutes. Turn the slices over and toast on the second side until golden brown, about 5 minutes longer. Remove from the oven and set aside. Leave the oven set at 450°F. While the bread is in the oven, use the large shredding holes on a box grater-shredder to shred the Gruyère cheese coarsely. You will need ½ cup (2 oz/60 g) well-packed cheese.

11 Adjust the seasonings

Taste the soup; it should be rich, meaty, and oniony, with pleasantly sweet overtones. If you feel the flavor lacks brightness, stir in a bit more salt or pepper until you achieve the flavor that you like. Keep in mind that the cheese that will top the soup is also salty.

12 Make the topping

Ladle the hot soup into 4 ovenproof bowls, filling each three-fourths full. Place 2 slices of toasted bread in the center of each bowl. Sprinkle the cheese on top of the bread, dividing it evenly. Carefully transfer the bowls to a rimmed baking sheet. Place in the oven and bake until the cheese is melted, 4–5 minutes. Using thick pot holders, transfer the hot bowls to saucers. Serve right away.

Finishing touches

A bowl of classic French Onion Soup topped with molten cheese is already delicious, but a hint of color here or a dash of texture there can improve the flavor even more. Presentations don't always have to be on top of the soup, however; an artistically folded napkin tucked between bowl and plate can bring out the color of the toasted cheese and transform an everyday soup into something special for guests.

Fresh thyme leaves (top left)
Leaving the woodier stem behind, pull off a few leaves of fresh thyme and sprinkle them on the cheese for a burst of color.

Balsamic syrup (left)
Place ½ cup (4 fl oz/125 ml) balsamic vinegar in a small saucepan over high heat. Simmer until syrupy, about 5 minutes. Let cool and drizzle over the cheese.

Folded napkin (above)
Spread the napkin flat and fold the corners to the center. Holding the center points in place, turn the napkin over. Fold the new corners to the center again. Turn the napkin over and pull each of the center points to the outside corners.

Minestrone

The word *minestrone* means "big soup," a perfect description for this chunky mixture of seasonal vegetables and pasta simmered in a full-flavored homemade stock. The vegetables are cooked until tender, but not for so long that they lose their identity, and the addition of pieces of cheese rind enriches the final flavor.

1 **Cook the vegetables**
Place a large, wide, heavy-bottomed saucepan over medium-low heat and add the olive oil. When the oil appears to shimmer, add the pancetta and cook, stirring, until it begins to shrivel, about 3 minutes. Add the onion, carrots, celery, and garlic and stir to coat with the oil. Cover the pan and cook until the vegetables are very soft but not browned, about 15 minutes.

2 **Simmer the soup**
Add the stock and the tomatoes, raise the heat to medium, and cook until large bubbles appear on the surface of the liquid. Stir in the Swiss chard, potato, green and wax beans, borlotti beans, cheese rind (if using), basil, parsley, salt, and pepper. Stir well to combine all the ingredients. Reduce the heat so that only small bubbles break the surface, cover the pan, and simmer until all the vegetables are soft, about 45 minutes. Preheat the oven to 200°F (95°C) and place individual bowls in the oven to warm.

3 **Add the pasta**
Stir the pasta into the soup and simmer gently, uncovered, until the pasta is tender and the soup has thickened, about 20 minutes; the timing depends on the pasta shape. Pasta with a hole in the center will cook more quickly than a solid pasta like orzo.

4 **Adjust the consistency of the soup**
The soup should be more soupy than stewlike. If the soup is too thick, add more stock or water, ½ cup (4 fl oz/125 ml) at a time, until the soup is the desired consistency. If it is too thin, raise the heat, bring the soup to a steady simmer, and cook, uncovered, until the liquid reduces slightly. This will thicken the soup.

5 **Adjust the seasonings**
Taste the soup. If it tastes dull, add more salt and pepper a little at a time, stirring and tasting after each addition, until the seasonings are to your liking.

6 **Serve the soup**
Ladle the soup into the warmed bowls and sprinkle with the freshly-grated cheese. Serve right away.

2 tablespoons extra-virgin olive oil

1 slice pancetta, about 1 oz (30 g), diced

1 medium yellow onion, diced (page 32)

2 carrots, peeled and diced (page 34)

2 stalks celery, diced (page 35)

1 teaspoon minced garlic (page 33)

6 cups (48 fl oz/1.5 l) Chicken Stock (page 18)

1½ lb (750 g) tomatoes, peeled, seeded, and diced (pages 36–37)

1 small bunch Swiss chard, stems removed and leaves torn into bite-sized pieces

1 Yukon gold potato, peeled and cut into ¼-inch (6-mm) dice

6 oz (185 g) green beans, trimmed and cut into ½-inch (12-mm) lengths

6 oz (185 g) yellow wax beans, trimmed and cut into ½-inch (12-mm) lengths

2 cups (14 oz/440 g) drained, canned borlotti or cannellini beans, rinsed

2 or 3 pieces Parmigiano-Reggiano cheese rind, optional

¼ cup (⅓ oz/10 g) chopped fresh basil (page 41)

¼ cup (⅓ oz/10 g) chopped fresh flat-leaf (Italian) parsley (page 41)

2 teaspoons kosher salt

⅛ teaspoon freshly ground pepper

½ cup (2½ oz/75 g) orzo, tubettini, or other tiny pasta shape

½ cup (2 oz/60 g) freshly grated Parmigiano Reggiano cheese

MAKES 6–8 SERVINGS

Borscht

This traditional Russian beet soup, ideally a vibrant ruby red, is complemented by a deep and richly flavored beef stock. The beets are first roasted to bring out their natural sugars. The addition of hearty cabbage and potatoes makes it a fitting dish to serve throughout the cold-weather months.

1½ lb (750 g) beets (about 3 medium), trimmed to leave ½ inch (12 mm) of the stem intact

2 tablespoons canola oil

1 leek, white and pale green parts, cut into slices ¼ inch (6 mm) thick (page 33)

1 parsnip, peeled and cut into ½-inch (12-mm) dice

1 large carrot, peeled and cut into ½-inch (12-mm) dice (page 34)

1 stalk celery, cut into ¼-inch (6-mm) dice (page 35)

1 tablespoon minced garlic (page 33)

6 cups (48 fl oz/1.5 l) Beef Stock (page 20) or Brown Beef Stock (page 22)

2 cups (12 oz/375 g) shredded cooked beef

2½ teaspoons kosher salt

¼ teaspoon freshly ground pepper

⅛ teaspoon ground allspice

2 cups (4 oz/125 g) chopped green cabbage

1 cup (6 oz/185 g) diced canned tomato

2 Yukon gold potatoes, peeled and each cut into 4 lengthwise wedges

2 tablespoons red wine vinegar

½ cup (4 oz/125 g) sour cream

1 tablespoon small fresh dill sprigs

MAKES 4 SERVINGS

SHORTCUT
You can either use leftovers from a roast beef dinner or buy 12 oz (375 g) of sliced roast beef from a neighborhood deli, dice it, and use for the borscht.

1 Prepare the beets
Preheat the oven to 350°F (180°C). Wrap each beet individually in a piece of aluminum foil. Place the foil-wrapped beets directly on the oven rack (or on a rimmed baking sheet) and roast until tender when pierced through the foil with the tip of a knife, about 1 hour. Remove the beets from the oven and let cool, still wrapped in the foil. When they are cool enough to handle, after about 15 minutes, unwrap the beets. Wear rubber gloves if you are concerned about staining your hands pink. Using the tip of a paring knife, lift off the skin and discard. Using the large shredding holes on a box grater-shredder, shred the beets into a bowl.

2 Simmer the soup base
Place a wide, heavy-bottomed saucepan over medium-low heat and add the oil. When the oil appears to shimmer, add the leek, parsnip, carrot, celery, and garlic and cook, stirring often, until tender, about 10 minutes. Add the stock, shredded beef, 2 teaspoons of the salt, the pepper, and the allspice. Bring to a boil over high heat. As soon as you see large bubbles begin to form, reduce the heat to low, cover, and cook until the vegetables are tender and the flavors are blended, 25–30 minutes. Stir in the shredded beets, cabbage, and tomato. Raise the heat to medium-low and cook, uncovered, until the cabbage is tender, about 10 minutes.

3 Cook the potatoes
Meanwhile, preheat the oven to 200°F (95°C) and place individual bowls in the oven to warm. Place the potatoes in a saucepan and add water to cover by 1 inch (2.5 cm) and the remaining ½ teaspoon salt. Cover the pan, place over high heat, and bring to a boil. Reduce the heat to medium-low and simmer until the potatoes are tender when pierced with the tip of a knife, about 15 minutes. Drain the potatoes, return them to the saucepan, cover, and keep warm.

4 Adjust the seasonings
Reduce the heat under the soup to low and stir in the vinegar. Taste the soup; if you feel it tastes a little dull, add a bit more vinegar, salt, or pepper. Add either seasoning a little at a time until the flavors are nicely balanced, keeping in mind that the potato and sour cream will mellow the flavors slightly.

5 Serve the soup
Divide the cooked potato wedges among the warmed bowls and ladle the hot soup over them, distributing the vegetables and beef evenly. Garnish each bowl with the sour cream and dill. Serve right away.

Manhattan Clam Chowder

Chowders are thick and chunky soups most often identified with seafood. Manhattan clam chowder stands out because it includes tomatoes in its clear broth instead of the more typical base of milk or cream. The tomatoes give the chowder a bright fresh flavor that supports the briny taste of the clams. The mollusks are steamed in an aromatic broth, which then becomes the foundation for the soup.

1 Make the clam broth
In a wide saucepan over high heat, combine the water, onion slice, celery, bay leaf, garlic clove, and salt and bring to a boil. Reduce the heat to low, cover, and cook for 20 minutes to blend the flavors.

2 Steam the clams in the broth
Discard any clams that do not close when gently tapped, then add the rest to the simmering broth. Raise the heat to medium-high, cover the pan, and steam the clams until they open: 3–4 minutes for littlenecks and 4–5 minutes for cherrystones. Using a slotted spoon, scoop out the opened clams and place them in a large bowl. Discard any clams that failed to open. Set a fine-mesh sieve over a 4-cup (32-fl oz/1-l) glass measuring cup. Line the sieve with a triple layer of damp cheesecloth (muslin). Ladle the broth through the sieve, leaving any sandy residue behind in the pan.

3 Remove the clams from their shells
Working over the bowl to capture any juices, pull the clam meats free with your fingers and place in a clean bowl. Discard the shells. Pour any juices left in the first bowl through the sieve, adding them to the cup with the strained broth. You will need 4 cups (32 fl oz/1 l) broth. If there is less, add water to make up the difference. Working over the clean bowl, snip the clams into ½-inch (12-mm) pieces with kitchen scissors. Cover the clams and refrigerate until needed.

4 Simmer the soup base
In a wide saucepan over medium-low heat, combine the bacon and olive oil and warm them until they sizzle. Add the diced onion, celery, and garlic and cook, stirring, until the vegetables are soft but not browned, about 12 minutes. Add the strained broth, tomatoes, minced parsley, thyme, salt, and pepper. Raise the heat to medium-high and bring to a boil. Stir in the barley, reduce the heat to low, cover, and cook until the barley is very soft, about 50 minutes.

5 Finish and serve the chowder
Preheat the oven to 200°F (95°C) and place individual bowls in the oven to warm. Uncover the pan and stir in the clams. Heat, stirring often, until the clams are heated through, about 3 minutes. Taste the soup; it should taste fresh, briny, and slightly tart. If it tastes dull, stir in more salt or pepper. Ladle the soup into the warmed bowls, garnished with the parsley leaves, and serve right away.

For the clam broth

3 cups (24 fl oz/750 ml) water

1 thick slice yellow onion

½ stalk celery with leaves

1 bay leaf

1 clove garlic, lightly crushed

1 teaspoon kosher salt

3 lb (750 g) cherrystone or littleneck clams, well scrubbed (page 39)

1 slice thick-cut lightly smoked bacon, cut into ¼-inch (6-mm) dice

1 tablespoon olive oil

½ cup (2½ oz/75 g) finely diced yellow onion (page 32)

1 stalk celery, diced (page 35)

1 large clove garlic, minced (page 33)

1 can (15½ oz/485 g) crushed plum (Roma) tomatoes with juice

1 tablespoon minced fresh flat-leaf (Italian) parsley (page 41), plus whole leaves for garnish

1 teaspoon fresh thyme leaves

½ teaspoon kosher salt

⅛ teaspoon freshly ground pepper

3 tablespoons pearl barley

MAKES 4 SERVINGS

4

Puréed Soups

A velvety texture and a satisfying mouthfeel characterize the best puréed soups. They are typically simple to make, drawing on a basketful of everyday vegetables, clear stocks, and the ease and speed of a food processor, blender, or food mill. They are also varied: some are perfectly smooth and others are lightly textured, some are piping hot and others are well chilled.

Carrot-Ginger Soup

A slow-simmered stock and fresh, firm carrots deliver a bright orange puréed soup with an intense sweet flavor, complemented by orange zest. The sweet onion, ginger, and garlic contribute pungency to the finished soup, while the starchy nature of the carrots delivers a pleasing spoon-coating consistency.

1 Combine the stock ingredients

If you need help making chicken stock, turn to page 18. In an 8-qt (8-l) heavy-bottomed pot, combine the chicken parts, onion, carrot, celery, garlic clove, parsley, bay leaf, and peppercorns. Add water just to cover the ingredients by 1 inch (2.5 cm).

2 Bring the stock to a boil

Place the pot over medium-high heat. Without stirring, slowly bring the liquid to a boil. As soon as you see large bubbles begin to form, reduce the heat until only small bubbles occasionally break the surface of the liquid. Use a large slotted spoon to skim the grayish foam that rises to the surface as the liquid reaches a boil, then continue skimming, without stirring, for the first 10 minutes.

3 Simmer the stock

Simmer the stock, uncovered, adjusting the heat periodically to keep the stock at a slow simmer, for 2–2½ hours, adding more water, if necessary, to keep the ingredients just covered. Do not stir, but continue to skim the surface every 30 minutes or so.

4 Strain the stock

Line a fine-mesh sieve with a triple layer of cheesecloth (muslin) that has been dampened and squeezed dry, and place it over a large bowl. Place the bowl in the sink, if you like, to make cleanup easier. Using a slotted spoon, remove the larger solids, then ladle or carefully pour the stock through the sieve. Discard the solids in the sieve.

5 Cool and defat the stock

If you are using the stock immediately, use a large spoon to skim and discard the fat from the surface of the stock, measure out 6 cups (48 fl oz/1.5 l), and proceed to step 6. If you are not using the stock right away, cool it in an ice bath until it is at least room temperature. Cover the stock and refrigerate it overnight. The next day, use a large spoon to lift off the fat solidified on the top. Measure out 6 cups (48 fl oz/1.5 l) of the stock and set it aside for the soup. Cover and refrigerate the remaining stock for up to 3 days or freeze for up to 3 months.

For the chicken stock

6 lb (3 kg) chicken backs and necks

1 large or 2 medium yellow onions, quartered through the stem end

1 large carrot, peeled and cut into 1-inch (2.5-cm) lengths

1 large stalk celery with leaves, cut into 1-inch (2.5-cm) lengths

1 clove garlic, peeled

3 or 4 sprigs fresh flat-leaf (Italian) parsley

1 bay leaf

8–10 whole peppercorns

1 large sweet onion such as Vidalia or Walla Walla

1 lb (500 g) carrots

2 cloves garlic

2-inch (5-cm) piece fresh ginger

1 orange

2 tablespoons unsalted butter

1 teaspoon kosher salt

⅛ teaspoon freshly ground pepper

Several blades of fresh chives

MAKES 4 SERVINGS

SHORTCUT

If you already have chicken stock on hand, use 6 cups (48 fl oz/1.5 l) prepared chicken stock and begin the recipe with step 6.

6>

6 Prepare the vegetables

First, dice the onion: Cut the onion in half lengthwise and peel each half. One at a time, place the onion halves, cut side down, on the cutting board. Make a series of lengthwise cuts perpendicular to the board, then a series of horizontal cuts with the knife blade parallel to the cutting board, and lastly cut crosswise to create ¼-inch (6-mm) dice. Be sure to stop just short of the root end; it holds the onion together as you cut. Next, slice the carrots: Peel the carrots, then cut them into slices ¼ inch thick. Finally, mince the garlic: Place the garlic cloves on a work surface, firmly press against them with the flat side of a knife, and pull away the papery skin. Mince the garlic. For more details on dicing onions and mincing garlic, turn to pages 32 and 33.

7 Prepare the ginger and orange zest

Using a paring knife or vegetable peeler, remove the thin beige skin from the fresh ginger, then use a rasp grater to grate enough ginger to measure 1½ teaspoons. Use the same fine rasps to grate ½ teaspoon zest from the orange. Make sure to grate only the colored portion of the orange peel, leaving the bitter white pith behind. Reserve the orange for another use.

CHEF'S TIP
When using citrus zest in recipes, such as this soup, add it near the end of the cooking time. This prevents the heat from causing the volatile—and flavorful—citrus oils to dissipate too quickly.

8 Sweat the vegetables

Place a heavy-bottomed pot over medium-low heat and add the butter. When the butter has melted and the foam begins to subside, add the onion and cook, stirring often, until it softens and is just translucent, about 10 minutes. You do not want the onion to take on any color. This process of slowly cooking the vegetables without letting them brown is called *sweating*. Add the garlic to the pot and cook, stirring, until it is fragrant, about 30 seconds. Add the carrots and salt to the pot and stir to coat the carrots well with the butter.

Simmer the soup

9 Add 2 cups (16 fl oz/500 ml) of the reserved stock to the pot. The stock should cover the carrots; if not, add more stock. Place the pot over high heat. As soon as you see large bubbles begin to form, reduce the heat until only small bubbles occasionally break the surface of the liquid and cover the pot. After a minute, check to make sure the stock is still at this gentle simmer. Re-cover and cook until the carrots are tender when pierced with the tip of a knife, about 20 minutes. Uncover and remove from the heat. Let the soup cool to lukewarm.

CHEF'S TIP

Because soups reduce in volume as they simmer, which concentrates their flavors, always season them at the end of cooking. If done at the beginning, you might end up with an overseasoned soup.

Purée the soup

10 Insert an immersion blender into the pot and purée the soup, moving the wand to ensure that all the ingredients are evenly puréed. Take care to immerse the blade completely to prevent spattering. (You can also use a food processor or blender for this step.) For more details on puréeing soups, turn to pages 42–43.

Finish the soup

11 Preheat the oven to 200°F (95°C) and place individual bowls in the oven to warm. Return the soup to medium-low heat and gradually whisk in the remaining 4 cups (32 fl oz/1 l) stock. Stir in the ginger and the orange zest. Reheat gently, stirring every now and again, until the soup is hot, about 10 minutes.

Adjust the seasonings

12 Add the pepper, then taste the soup. It should have a deep carrot flavor enhanced by onion and garlic, with accents of orange and ginger. If you feel the soup tastes dull, stir in a little more salt or pepper to perk up the flavors.

Serve the soup

13 Using kitchen scissors, snip the chives into tiny pieces. Ladle the soup into the warmed bowls and garnish with the chives. Serve right away.

Finishing touches

Thick and colorful puréed soups provide the perfect backdrop for decorative finishes. Against the backdrop of any bold-colored puréed soup, you can use lightly whisked plain yogurt or crème fraîche to produce professional-looking flourishes. Pour the ingredient into a locking plastic bag. Using scissors, snip off a corner of the bag, creating a small hole. The liquid will flow through to help you make interesting designs.

Zigzags (top left)
Using a smooth back-and-forth motion, move the snipped plastic bag containing the yogurt or crème fraîche above the surface of the soup to create a zigzag-patterned garnish.

Polka dots (left)
Holding it steady in one place, squeeze the plastic bag to create large and small polka dots over the surface of the soup.

Hearts (above)
Using a circular motion, squeeze the plastic bag to make several small spirals. Next, using a skewer or the tip of a paring knife, run the point through the center of the spiral to create heart shapes.

Puréed Vegetable Soup Variations

Now that you have made Carrot-Ginger Soup (page 69), you have learned the important technique of puréeing. Whenever you purée vegetables with stock or other liquid, you break them up into minute bits that are suspended in the liquid, transforming the two distinct elements into a thickened, smooth whole. The resulting soup is often already velvety, although sometimes cream or yogurt is whisked in at the end for a smoother consistency, as you'll see in some of these variations. You will also discover here that the varying starch content of vegetables means that the amount of liquid you will need differs from soup to soup. Each variation makes 4 to 6 servings.

Artichoke Soup

Here, puréed artichokes hearts are paired with salty prosciutto.

In a 3-qt (3-l) saucepan over medium heat, melt 3 tablespoons unsalted butter. Add ½ cup (2½ oz/75 g) finely chopped yellow onion and ½ cup (2½ oz/75 g) finely chopped celery and sauté until softened, 10–12 minutes. Add 2 minced garlic cloves and sauté for 1 minute. Add 3 cups (24 fl oz/750 ml) Chicken Stock (page 18), 1 bag (12 oz/375 g) thawed frozen artichoke hearts, 1 tablespoon fresh lemon juice, 1 teaspoon kosher salt, and ¼ teaspoon white pepper. Bring to a boil, reduce the heat to low, cover, and simmer until the artichokes are tender, about 20 minutes.

Meanwhile, in a small frying pan over medium heat, warm 2 tablespoons olive oil. Add 2 slices prosciutto cut into ¼-inch (6-mm) pieces. Sauté until the prosciutto is crisp, 4–5 minutes. Set aside.

Purée the soup, then stir in 1 cup (8 fl oz/ 250 ml) heavy (double) cream and heat through. Adjust the seasonings and serve right away, garnishing each serving with the prosciutto pieces, dividing evenly.

Curried Pea Soup

English peas and a little curry powder make a fresh-tasting puréed soup that can also be served cold.

In a 3-qt (3-l) saucepan over medium heat, melt 3 tablespoons unsalted butter. Add 1 cup (4 oz/125 g) chopped leek (white and pale green parts) and sauté until tender, 6–8 minutes. Sprinkle 2 teaspoons curry powder and 2 tablespoons all-purpose (plain) flour over the leeks and stir until well blended. Add 4 cups (32 fl oz/1 l) Chicken Stock (page 18), 5 cups (1½ lb/750 g) frozen petite peas or fresh English peas, 1 teaspoon kosher salt, and ⅛ teaspoon white pepper. Bring to a boil, reduce the heat to low, cover, and simmer until the peas are tender, about 15 minutes.

Purée the soup, then whisk in ½ cup (4 oz/125 g) plain yogurt until smooth and heat through. Adjust the seasonings and serve right away, garnishing each serving with 1 tablespoon plain yogurt.

Sweet Potato & Cumin Soup

The natural flavor of sweet potatoes, a favorite fall vegetable, is heightened by the addition of lime and cumin.

In a 3-qt (3-l) saucepan over medium heat, melt 3 tablespoons unsalted butter. Add ½ cup (2½ oz/75 g) chopped yellow onion and sauté until softened, 8–10 minutes. Add 2 minced garlic cloves and 2 teaspoons ground cumin and sauté for 1 minute. Add 3½ cups (28 fl oz/ 875 ml) Chicken Stock (page 18), 1½ lb (750 g) sweet potato pieces (½-inch/ 12-mm pieces), and ½ teaspoon kosher salt. Bring to a boil, reduce the heat to low, cover, and simmer until the potatoes are tender, about 20 minutes.

Purée the soup, then stir in 2 tablespoons fresh lime juice. Adjust the seasonings and serve right away, garnishing each serving with a sprinkle of chopped fresh cilantro (fresh coriander).

Roasted Butternut Squash Soup

Roasting the squash first makes this fall soup smoky and sweet, while the apple adds a touch of tartness.

Preheat the oven to 400°F (200°C), and pour 1½ cups (12 fl oz/375 ml) water into a baking pan. Cut a 2½-lb (1.25-kg) butternut squash in half lengthwise, discard the seeds, and rub the cut sides with 2 teaspoons olive oil. Place the squash, cut side down, in the pan and bake until the tip of a knife pierces the skin easily, 45–50 minutes. When cool enough to handle, scoop out the pulp; you should have about 3 cups (1½ lb/750 g).

Next, in a 3-qt (3-l) saucepan over medium heat, melt 3 tablespoons unsalted butter. Add 1 small chopped yellow onion and 1 peeled, cored, and chopped Granny Smith apple and sauté until softened, 10–12 minutes. Add 2 chopped garlic cloves and sauté for 1 minute. Add 2 cups (16 fl oz/500 ml) Chicken Stock (page 18), the squash pulp, 1 teaspoon kosher salt, and ¼ teaspoon white pepper. Bring to a boil, reduce the heat to low, cover, and simmer until slightly thickened, about 10 minutes.

Purée the soup, then stir in ¼ teaspoon ground coriander and ⅛ teaspoon ground nutmeg. Adjust the seasonings and serve right away, garnishing each serving with 1 tablespoon sour cream and a sprinkle of ground cinnamon.

Roasted Red Pepper Soup

This creamy red soup marries two summertime harvests, red bell peppers and fresh basil.

Preheat the broiler (grill) and line 2 large rimmed baking sheets with aluminum foil. Remove the stems from 5 large red bell peppers (capsicums) and cut the peppers lengthwise into sections along the natural seams. Remove the ribs and seeds and flatten the sections slightly with your hand. Lightly brush the peppers with olive oil and place skin side up on the prepared pans. Peel 1 yellow onion and cut it crosswise into 4 equal slices. Lightly brush with olive oil and arrange on the pans. Broil (grill) the vegetables, one pan at a time, until the pepper skins are charred all over and the onion slices have black specks on them, 6–8 minutes. Remove from the broiler, fold the foil around the peppers and onion and let stand for 10 minutes. Use a paring knife to scrape off the charred pepper skins and discard.

Next, in a 3-qt (3-l) saucepan, stir together 2 cups (16 fl oz/500 ml) Chicken Stock (page 18), the peppers and onion and any cooking juices, 2 minced garlic cloves, 2 tablespoons tomato paste, ½ teaspoon salt, and ¼ teaspoon red pepper flakes. Bring to a boil, reduce the heat to low, cover, and simmer until slightly thickened, about 15 minutes.

Purée the soup, then stir in 1 cup (8 fl oz/250 ml) heavy (double) cream and heat through. Adjust the seasonings and serve right away, garnishing each serving with a sprinkle of torn fresh basil.

Chestnut Soup

When making this soup, look for vacuum-packed chestnuts in 15–20 oz (470–625 g) jars. Because of their slightly mealy consistency, a food processor works better than an immersion blender for puréeing.

In a 3-qt (3-l) saucepan over medium heat, melt 3 tablespoons unsalted butter. Add 1 diced yellow onion and 1 diced celery stalk and sauté until softened, about 10 minutes. Add 3½ cups (28 fl oz/875 ml) Chicken Stock (page 18), 2 cups (16 oz/500 g) cooked, unsweetened peeled chestnuts, ½ teaspoon kosher salt, and ¼ teaspoon freshly ground pepper. Bring to a boil, reduce the heat to low, cover, and simmer until the chestnuts break up easily when pressed against the side of the pan, about 30 minutes.

Purée the soup in 2 batches in a food processor, pulsing to break up the chestnuts. Pour the soup through a medium-mesh sieve. Using the back of a ladle, push the solids through the sieve, extracting as much liquid as possible. Discard the solids.

Return the soup to the saucepan and stir in 1 cup (8 fl oz/250 ml) half-and-half (half cream) and 1 tablespoon brandy. Simmer until heated through. Adjust the seasonings and serve right away, garnishing each serving with a sprinkle of small croutons.

Tomato Soup

The best tomato soup has a smooth, velvety texture and a deep red color, which you can ensure by using the best tomatoes you can find during their peak season (June through September). Vegetable stock makes a medium-bodied, fresh-tasting soup, but chicken stock will deliver an extra layer of richness.

1 **Dice the vegetables**
If you need help dicing onions and celery or mincing garlic, turn to pages 32, 35, and 33. First, dice the onion: Cut the onion in half lengthwise and peel each half. One at a time, place the onion halves, cut side down, on the cutting board. Make a series of lengthwise cuts perpendicular to the board, then a series of horizontal cuts with the knife blade parallel to the cutting board, and lastly cut crosswise to create ¼-inch (6-mm) dice. Be sure to stop just short of the root end; it holds the onion together as you cut. Next, dice the celery: Cut the celery stalk lengthwise into strips ¼ inch wide, then cut the strips crosswise into ¼-inch dice. Finally, mince the garlic: Place the garlic clove on a work surface, firmly press against it with the flat side of a knife, and pull away the papery skin. Rock the knife rhythmically over the garlic to mince it.

2 **Peel the tomatoes**
Fill a large saucepan three-fourths full of water and bring it to a boil. While waiting for the water to boil, fill a large bowl three-fourths full of ice water. Use a paring knife to cut a small X in the blossom (bottom) end of each tomato, cutting through the skin but not too much into the flesh. Working in batches of 3 or 4 tomatoes at a time, use a slotted spoon to lower the tomatoes into the boiling water. Leave the tomatoes in the water for 10–15 seconds; the timing depends on the ripeness and size of the tomatoes. As soon as you see the tomato skin begin to curl at the X, use the slotted spoon to remove the tomatoes and immediately plunge them into the ice water to stop any further cooking. Leave the tomatoes in the water for about 20 seconds, then drain them. Starting at the X, peel away the skins from the tomatoes, using your fingers or a paring knife. To find out more about blanching and peeling tomatoes, turn to page 36.

3 **Core the tomatoes**
Using the tip of the knife, make a shallow circular cut in the stem end of each tomato to remove the green stem, taking care to remove as little of the flesh as possible. It is best to do this over a bowl so you can capture any juices. Leave the tomatoes whole.

1 yellow onion

1 stalk celery

1 clove garlic

1½ lb (750 g) plum (Roma) tomatoes

2 tablespoons extra-virgin olive oil

2 cups (16 fl oz/500 ml) Vegetable Stock (page 24) or Chicken Stock (page 18)

1 teaspoon kosher salt

⅛ teaspoon freshly ground pepper

½–1 teaspoon sugar, optional

1 tablespoon minced fresh flat-leaf (Italian) parsley

MAKES 4 SERVINGS

SHORTCUT
When tomatoes are not in season, you can substitute 1 can (28 oz/875 g) plum (Roma) tomatoes and the juices for the fresh tomatoes and skip to step 4.

4 Sweat the vegetables

Place a heavy-bottomed saucepan over medium-low heat and add the olive oil. When the oil appears to shimmer, add the onion, celery, and garlic and cook, stirring occasionally, until they soften, about 12 minutes. You don't want them to take on any color. This process of slowly cooking vegetables without letting them brown is called *sweating*.

5 Simmer the soup

Add 1 cup (8 fl oz/250 ml) of the stock, the tomatoes with their juices, and the salt to the saucepan. Raise the heat to medium-high and bring the soup to a boil. As soon as you see large bubbles begin to form, reduce the heat until only small bubbles occasionally break the surface of the liquid and cover the pan. After about 1 minute, check to make sure the stock is at this gentle simmer. Re-cover and cook until the tomatoes are very soft, about 25 minutes. Uncover the pan and remove it from the heat. Let the soup cool to lukewarm.

6 Purée the soup

If you are not sure how to purée in a blender or food processor, turn to page 42. Working in batches to ensure an even consistency, ladle the tomato mixture into a blender or food processor and purée; take care not to overfill the container as spattering can occur. Stop the machine occasionally to scrape down the sides with a narrow rubber spatula as necessary. Continue to process until the mixture is smooth, then return the purée to the pan. (You can also use an immersion blender to purée this soup; see page 43.)

7 Adjust the consistency

Preheat the oven to 200°F (95°C) and place individual bowls in the oven to warm. Return the soup to medium-low heat. The purée should have a good spoon-coating consistency. However, the moisture content of tomatoes can vary, so you will probably need to adjust the consistency. To do so, whisk in as much of the remaining 1 cup (8 fl oz/250 ml) stock as needed to achieve the desired consistency. Reheat gently, stirring every now and again, until the soup is hot, about 10 minutes.

8 Adjust the seasonings

Add the pepper, then taste the soup. Tomatoes, depending on variety and/or growing conditions, can be too acidic—in other words, they sometimes taste as sour as lemon juice. To eliminate this unwanted tartness, add ½ teaspoon sugar, stir well, taste again, and add more if needed. Do not be tempted to add too much. A little acidity gives the soup a pleasant brightness and you don't want the soup to taste sweet. Taste for salt at the same time and add more, a small amount at a time, until the flavors are nicely balanced.

9 Serve the soup

Ladle the soup into the warmed bowls and garnish with the minced parsley. Serve right away.

Tomato Soup Variations

Because tomato season is short, it sometimes flies by before I get a chance to make tomato soup. If that happens, I don't despair, as I've discovered that quality canned tomatoes make a delicious soup, too (see Shortcut, page 77). Look for tomatoes that are whole, in their own juices, and don't have any seasonings, like basil, added to them. That way, you can adjust the flavor to your own preference. Now that you know how to work with tomatoes, try these three variations that show you how to prepare different-textured soups from the puréed tomato base. Each variation makes 4 to 6 servings.

Cream of Tomato Soup

The only changes you need to make to the original soup for this rich version are to reduce the stock and add heavy cream to the base.

Follow the recipe to make Tomato Soup, using only 1 cup (8 fl oz/250 ml) Vegetable Stock or Chicken Stock.

In step 7, adjust the consistency of the puréed soup by gradually stirring in 1 cup (8 fl oz/250 ml) heavy (double) cream, then reheat gently. Do not let the soup boil.

Adjust the seasonings. Serve right away.

> **CHEF'S TIP**
> *To make your own bread crumbs, dry slices of French, Italian, or whole-wheat (wholemeal) bread on a baking sheet in a 200°F (95°C) oven for about 1 hour. Let the slices cool, break them into small pieces, and then pulse them in a food processor until they are reduced to fine or coarse crumbs as needed.*

Chunky Tomato Soup

Altering the texture of the original soup by puréeing only part of it gives you a thicker soup with juicy pieces of tomato in every spoonful.

Peel and core 1½ lb (750 g) plum (Roma) tomatoes, then cut them in half through their equator. One at a time, cut the tomato halves into ½-inch (12-mm) dice.

In a heavy-bottomed saucepan over medium-low heat, warm 2 tablespoons extra-virgin olive oil. Add 1 diced yellow onion, 1 diced celery stalk, and 1 minced garlic clove and sauté until softened, about 12 minutes. Add 1 cup (8 fl oz/ 250 ml) Vegetable Stock (page 24) or Chicken Stock (page 18), 1 teaspoon kosher salt, and the diced tomatoes. Bring to a boil, then reduce the heat and simmer until the tomatoes are very soft, about 25 minutes. Let cool to lukewarm.

Purée 1 cup (8 fl oz/250 ml) of the soup, then stir it into the remaining soup and reheat gently. Stir in ½ teaspoon grated orange zest and adjust the seasonings. Serve right away.

Pappa al Pomodoro
Italian Tomato & Bread Soup

Adding whole-wheat bread crumbs to Tomato Soup results in a Tuscan classic. *Pappa* means "mush," which aptly describes this comforting soup.

Peel and core 1½ lb (750 g) plum (Roma) tomatoes. In a heavy-bottomed saucepan over medium-low heat, warm ¼ cup (2 fl oz/60 ml) extra-virgin olive oil. Add 1 diced yellow onion, 1 diced celery stalk, and 3 minced garlic cloves and sauté until softened, about 12 minutes. Add 1 cup (8 fl oz/250 ml) Vegetable Stock (page 24) or Chicken Stock (page 18), 1 teaspoon kosher salt, and the tomatoes. Bring to a boil, then reduce the heat and simmer until the tomatoes are very soft, about 25 minutes. Let cool to lukewarm.

Purée the soup, then return it to the pan. Stir in 2½ cups (10 oz/315 g) coarse dried whole-wheat (wholemeal) bread crumbs and reheat gently. Stir in ¼ cup (⅓ oz/ 10 g) torn fresh basil leaves and adjust the seasonings. Serve right away.

Potato-Leek Soup

Make this soup in cool-weather months, when both potatoes and leeks are at their best. The slowly cooked leeks and onion add a natural sweetness to the soup, while the starchy character of the potatoes gives it wonderful body. Use only russet potatoes for this soup; other varieties lack the starch required to achieve proper consistency.

1 Prepare the leeks and onion
For more details on preparing leeks, turn to page 33. Place the leeks on a cutting board and trim off the root ends and the dark portion of the green tops. Halve each leek lengthwise, then place cut side down on the cutting board and halve lengthwise again. Rinse thoroughly in a large bowl or basin of cool water, gently separating the layers of leaves as needed to remove any dirt lodged between them. Drain well. Working in batches, gather the leek leaves together and cut crosswise into slices ⅛ inch (3 mm) thick. You should have about 6 cups (18 oz/560 g) sliced leeks. Next, cut the onion in half lengthwise through the stem end and peel each half. Place the onion halves, cut side down, on the cutting board. Slice each half into thin half-moons.

2 Prepare the potatoes
Peel the potatoes with a vegetable peeler or paring knife. Cut each potato lengthwise into slices ¼ inch (6 mm) thick. Stack 2 or 3 slices on top of one another and cut the potatoes lengthwise into strips ¼ inch wide. Then cut the stack crosswise at ¼-inch intervals to create ¼-inch dice. Repeat with the remaining potatoes.

3 Sweat the vegetables
Place a wide saucepan over medium-low heat and add the butter. When the butter has melted and the foam begins to subside, add the leeks and onion. Using a wooden spoon or a heatproof spatula, stir the leeks and onion to coat them with the butter. Cover and cook until the leeks and onion are very tender, about 15 minutes. Check every few minutes to make sure the vegetables are not sticking to the pan bottom. You don't want them to color. This process of cooking vegetables slowly without letting them brown is called *sweating*.

4 Simmer the soup
Add 4 cups (32 fl oz/1 l) of the stock, the potatoes, and the salt to the pan. Raise the heat to medium-high and bring to a boil. As soon as you see large bubbles begin to form, reduce the heat until only small bubbles occasionally break the surface of the liquid and cover the pan. After about 1 minute, check to make sure the stock is at this gentle simmer. Re-cover and cook until the potatoes are tender when pierced with the tip of a knife, about 15 minutes. Uncover the pot and remove it from the heat. Let the soup cool to lukewarm.

5 or 6 large leeks

1 large yellow onion

1 lb (500 g) russet potatoes

3 tablespoons unsalted butter

4–5 cups (32–40 fl oz/1–1.25 l) Chicken Stock (page 18)

1 teaspoon salt

⅛ teaspoon freshly ground pepper

Several blades fresh chives

MAKES 6 SERVINGS

CHEF'S TIP
Don't be tempted to substitute another variety of potato here. Most puréed potato-based soups rely on the low moisture and high starch content of russet potatoes (also called Idaho potatoes) for their smooth, thick consistency.

5 Purée the soup

If you are not sure how to purée in a blender or food processor, turn to page 42. Working in batches to ensure an even consistency, ladle the potato mixture into a blender or food processor and purée; take care not to overfill the container, as spattering can occur. Stop the machine occasionally to scrape down the sides with a narrow rubber spatula as necessary. Continue to process until the mixture is smooth, then return the purée to the pan. (You can also use an immersion blender to purée this soup; see page 43.)

6 Adjust the consistency

Preheat the oven to 200°F (95°C) and place individual bowls in the oven to warm. Return the soup to medium-low heat. The purée should have the consistency of heavy (double) cream. However, potatoes absorb varying amounts of liquid depending on their age, so you will probably need to adjust the consistency. To do so, gradually whisk in as much of the remaining 1 cup (8 fl oz/250 ml) stock as needed to achieve a good spoon-coating consistency. Reheat gently, stirring frequently, until visibly steaming, about 10 minutes.

7 Adjust the seasonings

Stir in the pepper, then taste the soup. It should taste primarily of the potatoes and oniony leeks, with an underlying richness from the chicken stock. If you feel the soup lacks depth, stir in a little more salt or pepper until the flavors are nicely balanced.

8 Serve the soup

Using kitchen scissors, snip the chives into ¼- to ½-inch (6- to 12-mm) pieces. Ladle the soup into the warmed bowls. Garnish each bowl with the chive pieces and serve right away.

> **CHEF'S TIP**
> *Potato-leek soup is also delicious served cold as vichyssoise. Transfer it to a large bowl, then cover and refrigerate until fully chilled, about 4 hours. Serve the soup in chilled bowls garnished with the chives. Because the cold air of the refrigerator often dulls the flavors of food, it is a good idea to taste and adjust the seasonings again before serving the cold soup.*

Potato-Leek Soup Variations

Having mastered the making of Potato-Leek Soup (page 81), you now have the confidence to transform this classic recipe into a trio of different soups, one that includes celery root and another made rich with the addition of tangy sharp Cheddar cheese. In both cases, you will need to sweat the aromatic vegetables, purée the base, and adjust the consistency so that the soup nicely coats a spoon. The third variation, however, skips the puréeing step in favor of a more rustic finish. You can also make any of these recipes vegetarian by substituting Vegetable Stock (page 24) for the Chicken Stock. Each variation makes 4 to 6 servings.

Potato-Cheese Soup

Add sharp Cheddar cheese, pungent dry mustard, and smoky paprika to make a potato soup brimming with robust and warming flavors.

In a wide saucepan over medium-low heat, melt 3 tablespoons unsalted butter. Add 6 cups (18 oz/560 g) thinly sliced leeks (white and pale green parts) and 1 sliced large yellow onion and sweat until tender, about 15 minutes. Add 4 cups (32 fl oz/1 l) Chicken Stock (page 18), 1 lb (500 g) peeled and diced russet potatoes, and 1 teaspoon salt and bring to a boil. Reduce the heat to low, cover, and simmer until the potatoes are tender, about 15 minutes. Let cool to lukewarm.

Purée the soup, then return it to the pan. Stir in 1½ cups (6 oz/185 g) coarsely shredded Cheddar cheese and 1 teaspoon dry mustard. Reheat gently, then adjust the consistency with up to 1 cup (8 fl oz/250 ml) Chicken Stock. Adjust the seasonings and serve right away, garnishing each serving with 2 teaspoons coarsely shredded Cheddar cheese and a sprinkle of sweet paprika.

Potato–Celery Root Soup

Because celery root quickly turns brown after cutting, you must immediately immerse it in water to which lemon juice has been added.

Trim and peel 1½ lb (750 g) celery root (celeriac) and cut it into ¼-inch (6-mm) cubes; put the cubes into a bowl filled with water and the juice of ½ lemon.

In a wide saucepan over medium-low heat, melt 3 tablespoons unsalted butter. Add 6 cups (18 oz/560 g) thinly sliced leeks (white and pale green parts) and 1 sliced large yellow onion and sweat until tender, about 15 minutes. Add 4 cups (32 fl oz/1 l) Chicken Stock (page 18), the drained celery root, and 1 teaspoon salt and bring to a boil. Reduce the heat to low, cover, and simmer for 10 minutes. Add 1 lb (500 g) peeled and diced russet potatoes, cover, and simmer until the potatoes and celery root are tender, about 15 minutes. Let cool to lukewarm.

Purée 3 cups (24 fl oz/750 ml) of the soup, then return it to the pan with 1 teaspoon dried tarragon. Reheat gently, then adjust the consistency with up to 1 cup (8 fl oz/250 ml) Chicken Stock. Adjust the seasonings and serve right away, garnishing each serving with chopped fresh chives.

Chunky Potato-Leek Soup

By simply changing how the onion is cut and not puréeing the base, a thick and hearty soup results.

In a wide saucepan over medium-low heat, melt 3 tablespoons unsalted butter. Add 6 cups (18 oz/560 g) thinly sliced leeks (white and pale green parts) and 1 diced large yellow onion (¼-inch/6-mm dice) and sweat until tender, about 15 minutes. Add 4 cups (32 fl oz/1 l) Chicken Stock (page 18), 1 lb (500 g) peeled and diced russet potatoes, and 1 teaspoon salt and bring to a boil. Reduce the heat to low, cover, and simmer until the potatoes are tender, about 15 minutes.

Adjust the seasonings and serve right away, garnishing each serving with chopped fresh chives.

White Bean Soup

Some of the cooked beans in this thick, creamy soup are puréed to give it body, while the rest are left whole, lending a rustic texture. The pancetta delivers both richness and meaty flavor, while the carrot and tomato provide flavor, color, and texture. Look for dried beans labeled "new crop," indicating they have been harvested within the past year, or, lacking labels, shop at a store with good turnover.

1 Soak the beans
Place the beans in a large sieve and rinse thoroughly under running cold water. Pick them over to remove any stones or discolored beans. Place in a bowl, add cold water to cover by 2 inches (5 cm), and let soak overnight in the refrigerator to rehydrate the dried beans.

2 Cook the vegetables with the pancetta
Place a large, wide saucepan over medium-low heat and add the olive oil. When the oil appears to shimmer, add the onion, celery, garlic, and pancetta and cook, stirring occasionally, until the onion has softened, about 12 minutes.

3 Cook the beans
Drain the beans, then add them to the pan with the water, stock, carrot, bay leaf, and sage. Bring to a boil over medium heat, using a large spoon to skim the foam that rises to the surface as the liquid reaches a boil. As soon as you see large bubbles begin to form, reduce the heat until only small bubbles occasionally break the surface. Simmer gently, uncovered, stirring occasionally, until the beans are tender. Begin testing the beans for doneness after about 1 hour, and then test every 15 minutes or so. In 1–1½ hours, the beans should be soft throughout, with no firmness or chalkiness at the center. If the soup becomes too thick before the beans cook through, stir in more water or stock, 1 cup (8 fl oz/250 ml) at a time.

4 Purée part of the soup
Lift the carrot from the pan and reserve. Discard the bay leaf. (The sage will be puréed with the soup.) Using a slotted spoon, transfer about 3 cups (21 oz/ 655 g) of the beans to a bowl, then transfer about ½ cup (4 fl oz/125 ml) of their liquid. Let cool to lukewarm. Ladle the cooled beans and liquid into a blender or food processor and purée until smooth. If you are not sure how to purée in a blender or food processor, turn to page 42. Return the purée to the pan with the remaining beans and place the pan over medium-low heat. Preheat the oven to 200°F (95°C) and place individual bowls in the oven to warm. Cut the carrot into ½-inch (12-mm) dice and add it to the soup with the tomato, salt, and pepper. Reheat gently over medium-low heat, stirring occasionally to prevent sticking, until hot, about 10 minutes.

5 Adjust the seasonings and serve the soup
Taste the soup; if you feel it tastes dull, stir in a little more salt or pepper until it is nicely balanced. Ladle into the warmed bowls and serve right away.

2¼ cups (1 lb/500 g) dried cannellini or Great Northern beans

2 tablespoons extra-virgin olive oil

1 yellow onion, diced (page 32)

1 stalk celery, diced (page 35)

1 tablespoon minced garlic (page 33)

1 slice pancetta, about 1 oz (30 g), diced

5 cups (40 fl oz/1.25 l) water

5 cups (40 fl oz/1.25 l) Chicken Stock (page 18)

1 large carrot, peeled

1 bay leaf

2 fresh sage leaves

1 fresh or canned tomato, peeled and diced (pages 36–37)

2 teaspoons kosher salt

⅛ teaspoon freshly ground pepper

MAKES 6–8 SERVINGS

CHEF'S TIP
Fried herb leaves are an easy and visually appealing garnish for soups. In a frying pan over medium heat, warm 3 tablespoons olive oil. Add the herb leaves (for example, sage, as pictured above) and cook, without stirring, until they crisp slightly, 2–3 minutes. Drain the herbs on paper towels before using.

White Bean Soup Variations

White Bean Soup (page 85) teaches you how to soak, cook, and purée beans for a soup that is an intriguing mix of smooth and chunky. But you can use these same lessons to make a perfectly smooth soup by puréeing all of the beans, rather than only a portion, as I do in the Split Pea Soup. This technique can also be applied to any of these variations for a more refined texture. Beans are a good match with a wide variety of flavorings—chiles, curry powder, smoked ham, garlicky sausage—as these six recipes prove. When time is short, make the soups that call for lentils or split peas, which don't require soaking. Each variation makes 4 to 6 servings.

White Bean Soup with Chard

Bite-sized pieces of chard simmered until tender add an earthiness to bean soup.

Pick over 2¼ cups (1 lb/500 g) dried cannellini or Great Northern beans and let soak overnight. Drain well.

In a large, wide saucepan over medium-low heat, warm 2 tablespoons extra-virgin olive oil. Add 1 diced yellow onion, 1 diced celery stalk, 1 tablespoon minced garlic, and 1 diced pancetta slice (about 1 oz/ 30 g) and sauté until softened, about 12 minutes. Add 5 cups (40 fl oz/1.25 l) *each* water and Chicken Stock (page 18), the drained beans, 1 large peeled carrot, 1 bay leaf, and 2 fresh sage leaves and bring to a boil. Reduce the heat to low and simmer until the beans are tender, 1–1½ hours.

Lift out the carrot and dice it. Discard the bay leaf. Purée 3 cups (21 oz/655 g) of the beans with ½ cup (4 fl oz/125 ml) of the cooking liquid, then return it to the pan. Add 4 cups (12 oz/375 g) firmly packed Swiss chard pieces (½-inch/12-mm pieces) and the carrot. Cover and simmer until the chard is tender, 10–15 minutes. Adjust the seasonings and serve right away.

Vegetarian White Bean Soup

This full-flavored vegetarian variation is seasoned with green chiles and cumin.

Pick over 2¼ cups (1 lb/500 g) dried cannellini or Great Northern beans and let soak overnight. Drain well.

In a large, wide saucepan over medium-low heat, warm 2 tablespoons extra-virgin olive oil. Add 1 diced yellow onion, 1 diced celery stalk, and 1 tablespoon minced garlic and sauté until softened, about 12 minutes. Add 5 cups (40 fl oz/1.25 l) *each* water and Vegetable Stock (page 24), the drained beans, 1 large peeled carrot, and 1 bay leaf and bring to a boil. Reduce the heat to low and simmer until the beans are tender, 1–1½ hours.

Lift out the carrot and dice it. Discard the bay leaf. Purée 3 cups (21 oz/655 g) of the beans with ½ cup (4 fl oz/125 ml) of the cooking liquid, then return it to the pan. Add 1 can (7 oz/220 g) diced green chiles with their liquid, 2 teaspoons ground cumin, 1 teaspoon fresh lime juice, ½ teaspoon salt, ½ teaspoon green hot-pepper sauce, and the carrot. Simmer for about 10 minutes. Adjust the seasonings and serve right away, garnishing lightly with chopped fresh cilantro (fresh coriander).

Curried Lentil Soup

This quick and easy soup calls for lentils, which don't need soaking.

Pick over 2¼ cups (1 lb/500 g) brown lentils and rinse under running cold water. Drain well.

In a large, wide saucepan over medium-low heat, melt 3 tablespoons unsalted butter. Add 2 cups (8 oz/250 g) diced yellow onion, ½ cup (2½ oz/75 g) diced carrot, and 1 tablespoon minced garlic and sauté until softened, about 12 minutes. Add 2 tablespoons Madras curry powder and ¼ teaspoon red pepper flakes and cook for 1 minute. Add the lentils, 5 cups (40 fl oz/1.25 l) *each* water and Chicken Stock (page 18), 1 bay leaf, and 2 tablespoons tomato paste and bring to a boil. Reduce the heat to low and simmer, uncovered, stirring, until the lentils are tender, about 40 minutes.

Discard the bay leaf. Purée 3 cups (21 oz/655 g) of the lentils with ½ cup (4 fl oz/125 ml) of the cooking liquid, then return it to the pan. Add 1 teaspoon salt and simmer for 10–12 minutes. Adjust the seasonings and serve right away, garnishing each serving with a dollop of plain yogurt and a sprinkle of chopped fresh cilantro (fresh coriander).

Split Pea Soup

In this smooth, thick soup, peas and smoky ham are paired to make a classic dish.

Pick over 2¼ cups (1 lb/500 g) split peas and rinse under running cold water. Drain well.

In a large, wide saucepan over medium-low heat, warm 2 tablespoons olive oil. Add 1 cup (4 oz/125 g) chopped yellow onion, ½ cup (2½ oz/75 g) chopped celery, and 1 tablespoon minced garlic and sauté until softened, about 12 minutes. Add the split peas, 4 cups (32 fl oz/1 l) *each* water and Chicken Stock (page 18), 1 bay leaf, and 1 whole peeled carrot and bring to a boil. Reduce the heat to low and simmer, uncovered, stirring occasionally, until the peas are tender, about 1 hour.

Lift out the carrot and dice it. Discard the bay leaf. Working in batches, purée all of the soup and return it to the pan. Add 1½ cups (9 oz/280 g) diced smoked ham, 1 teaspoon salt, ¼ teaspoon freshly ground pepper, and the carrot. Gently heat the soup until the ham is heated through. Adjust the seasonings and serve right away.

SHORTCUT
If you don't have time to soak beans overnight, try this shortcut: Put the beans in a deep pot, add water to cover by 3–4 inches (7.5–10 cm), and bring to a simmer. Remove the pot from the heat, cover, and let stand for 1 hour.

Black Bean Soup

Chipotle chiles (smoke-dried jalapeños) packed in adobo sauce provide piquancy to this simple version of Mexican black bean soup.

Pick over 2¼ cups (1 lb/500 g) dried black beans and let soak overnight. Drain well.

In a large, wide saucepan over medium-low heat, sauté ½ lb (250 g) diced thick-cut lightly smoked bacon (½-inch/12-mm pieces) until cooked but not crisp, about 6 minutes. Drain on paper towels; reserve. Add 1 cup (4 oz/125 g) chopped yellow onion, ½ cup (2½ oz/75 g) chopped celery, and 1 tablespoon minced garlic to the pan and sauté until softened, about 10 minutes. Add the drained black beans, 5 cups (40 fl oz/1.25 l) *each* water and Beef Stock (page 20), 1 bay leaf, 4 fresh thyme sprigs, and 1 minced chipotle chile with 1 teaspoon adobo sauce and bring to a boil. Reduce the heat to low and simmer, uncovered, stirring occasionally, until the beans are tender, 1½–2 hours.

Discard the thyme and bay leaf. Purée 3 cups (21 oz/655 g) of the beans with ½ cup (4 fl oz/125 ml) of the cooking liquid, then return it to the pan. Add ½ cup (3 oz/90 g) diced canned tomato, the reserved bacon pieces, ½ teaspoon salt, and ¼ teaspoon freshly ground pepper and gently heat through. Adjust the seasonings and serve right away, garnishing each serving with 1 tablespoon sour cream.

Three-Bean Soup with Linguiça

Choose either mild or hot Portuguese linguiça sausage to suit your palate when making this warming bean soup.

Pick over ¾ cup (5 oz/155 g) *each* dried pink beans, cannellini beans, and chickpeas (garbanzo beans) and let soak overnight. Drain well.

In a large, wide saucepan over medium-low heat, warm 2 tablespoons olive oil. Add 1 cup (4 oz/125 g) chopped yellow onion, ½ cup (2½ oz/75 g) chopped celery, 1 tablespoon minced garlic, and 1 seeded and chopped small red bell pepper (capsicum) and sauté until softened, about 5 minutes. Add the drained beans, 5 cups (40 fl oz/1.25 l) *each* water and Chicken Stock (page 18), 1 bay leaf, and 1 whole peeled carrot and bring to a boil. Reduce the heat to low and simmer, uncovered, stirring occasionally, until the beans are tender, 1½–2 hours.

Lift out the carrot and dice it. Discard the bay leaf. Purée 3 cups (21 oz/655 g) of the beans with ½ cup (4 fl oz/125 ml) of their cooking liquid, then return it to the pan. Add 5 oz (155 g) linguiça sausage pieces (¼-inch/6-mm pieces), 1 cup (6 oz/185 g) chopped fresh or canned tomatoes, 1 teaspoon dried marjoram, ½ teaspoon smoked paprika, ½ teaspoon salt, ¼ teaspoon freshly ground pepper, and the carrot and gently heat through. Adjust the seasonings and serve right away.

Gazpacho

This gazpacho tastes like a bountiful summertime garden, rich with the flavors of vine-ripened tomatoes and freshly picked bell peppers and cucumbers. The color is bright and intense, yet another reflection of the season. Ideally, the puréed soup should rest overnight in the refrigerator, which allows time for the flavors to blend and deepen.

2 slices day-old coarse Italian bread, about ½ inch (12 mm) thick

1 cup (8 fl oz/250 ml) water

3 lb (1.5 kg) fresh Roma (plum) tomatoes, peeled (page 36) and halved lengthwise

1 yellow onion, diced (page 32)

1 yellow or green bell pepper (capsicum), seeded (page 36) and diced

1 English (hothouse) cucumber, peeled and diced

1 tablespoon minced garlic (page 33)

⅓ cup (3 fl oz/80 ml) extra-virgin olive oil

3 tablespoons red wine vinegar

1 teaspoon kosher salt

⅛ teaspoon freshly ground pepper

For the croutons

¼ cup (2 fl oz/60 ml) extra-virgin olive oil

2 slices coarse Italian bread, about ½ inch (12 mm) thick, cut into ½-inch cubes

MAKES 6 SERVINGS

CHEF'S TIP

If your tomatoes aren't yet ripe, place them on a sunny windowsill or in a paper bag with a pear or banana for 2 or 3 days. The pear or banana will give off ethylene gas, naturally hastening ripening. Ripe tomatoes will give slightly when lightly pressed with your fingertips. Do not store tomatoes in the refrigerator. The cold turns them mealy and diminishes their flavor.

1 Soak the bread
In a large bowl, combine the bread slices and water. Let the mixture stand for 5 minutes, then pour the contents of the bowl into a sieve and discard the water. Squeeze the bread with your hands to remove excess moisture. The bread will help thicken the soup to the right consistency.

2 Prepare the tomatoes
If you need help seeding and dicing tomatoes, turn to page 37. Set a fine-mesh sieve over a bowl and use your fingers to scoop the seed sacs from the tomato halves into the sieve. Using the back of a large spoon, press down on the seeds and pulp to extract as much juice as possible. Discard the solids. Using a paring knife, make a V-shaped cut to remove the green tomato stem from each half. Then, one at a time, place the halves, cut side down, on a cutting board and make a series of lengthwise cuts, about ¼ inch (6 mm) apart. Line up the ¼-inch strips and cut them crosswise into ¼-inch dice. Reserve ½ cup (3 oz/ 90 g) diced tomatoes in a small bowl. Add the remainder to the bowl with the reserved juices; you should have about 5 cups (30 oz/940 g) chopped tomatoes.

3 Purée the ingredients
Add ¼ cup (1 oz/30 g) *each* of the chopped onion, pepper, and cucumber to the reserved ½ cup diced tomatoes, stir lightly, cover, and refrigerate until serving. Add the remaining chopped vegetables, the garlic, and the soaked bread to the bowl with the tomatoes and juices and stir well. Working in batches, ladle the mixture into a blender or food processor and process to a smooth purée. For more information on puréeing soups, turn to page 42. Pour the purée into a tall glass pitcher and stir in the olive oil, vinegar, salt, and pepper. Cover and refrigerate for several hours or up to overnight to allow the flavors the blend.

4 Make the croutons
Place a heavy-bottomed frying pan over medium-low heat and add the olive oil. When the oil appears to shimmer, add the bread cubes and cook, turning the cubes as they color and adding more oil as needed, until golden on all sides, about 10 minutes. Transfer to a plate.

5 Serve the soup
Put individual bowls in the refrigerator for about 10 minutes to chill. Taste the soup. If it tastes dull, stir in a bit more vinegar, salt, or pepper until it is to your liking. Pour the soup into the chilled bowls. Top each serving with croutons and the reserved vegetables, dividing them evenly. Serve right away.

5

Cream Soups
& Chowders

The secrets to the thick and creamy soups you'll find in this chapter are the careful addition of cream, cooked rice, or cubed potatoes. These thickeners are what give cream soups and chowders their signature silky texture, satisfying mouthfeel, and rich taste. You will also uncover the key to making a roux, the mixture of butter and flour that contributes body to many cream soups.

Cream of Broccoli Soup

Fresh, bright green broccoli, which is at its best from fall through spring, gives this cream soup a full flavor and a warm, pleasing color. The rich stock, whole milk, cream, and a simple roux all help to create the lightly thickened consistency and smooth texture that mark the best cream soups.

1 Prepare the broccoli

Place the broccoli on a cutting board and, using a chef's knife, trim off 1 inch (2.5 cm) from the bottom of each stalk and discard. Using a vegetable peeler or paring knife, peel the tough outer layer from the remaining broccoli stalks. Using the chef's knife, cut off the florets from the tops of the stalks. Chop the florets into ½-inch (12-mm) pieces. Next, coarsely chop the stalks. Measure the chopped florets and stalks. You should have about 6 cups (12 oz/375 g).

2 Steam the broccoli

Fill a wide-bottomed saucepan with ½ inch (12 mm) of water and bring to a boil over high heat. Place a collapsible metal steamer basket in the pan. Check to make sure that the water is not touching the bottom of the basket. Arrange the broccoli in an even layer in the basket. Cover and let the broccoli cook in the steam for 5 minutes. Uncover and test the broccoli with the tip of a paring knife; it should be bright green and tender enough for the knife to pierce easily. If it is not, continue to steam for another minute or two until it is tender. Using an oven mitt to protect your hand, lift out the steamer basket and place it on a plate. Let the broccoli cool to lukewarm, about 5 minutes.

3 Purée the broccoli

Set aside ¼ cup (½ oz/15 g) of the smallest, nicest-looking floret pieces for garnish, if desired (see page 97). Transfer the remaining broccoli to a food processor and process until finely chopped. Remove the blade from the processor. Use a narrow rubber spatula to scrape out the broccoli from the food processor into a glass measuring cup. You should have about 2 cups (16 fl oz/500 ml) puréed broccoli. ⟩

1 bunch broccoli, about 1¼ lb (625 g)

2 cups (16 fl oz/500 ml) whole milk, plus 1 cup (8 fl oz/250 ml) for thinning, if needed

2 cups (16 fl oz/500 ml) Chicken Stock (page 18) or Vegetable Stock (page 24)

3 tablespoons unsalted butter

3 tablespoons all-purpose (plain) flour

1 teaspoon kosher salt

⅛ teaspoon freshly ground pepper

½ cup (4 fl oz/125 ml) heavy (double) cream

MAKES 4 SERVINGS

CHEF'S TIP
Many cooks discard the broccoli stalks after cutting off the prized florets. Although not as pretty, peeled broccoli stalks are delicious puréed in soups (as shown here), cooked in stir-fries, or shaved raw for salads.

Heat the liquids

4 Pour the milk and stock into separate small saucepans and place them over low heat. Heat the milk and the stock just until small bubbles form around the edge of the pan, then remove them from the heat. You do not want the liquids to boil, or their intense heat could affect the texture of the roux.

Make the roux

5 To find out more about making a roux, turn to page 40. Place a heavy-bottomed saucepan over medium-low heat and add the butter. When the butter has melted and the foam begins to subside, sprinkle the flour evenly over the butter. Stir with a heatproof spatula or wooden spoon until the flour is completely blended with the butter and no lumps of flour are visible, about 2 minutes.

Add the liquids to the roux

6 Gradually add the hot milk to the roux while stirring gently with a small whisk to dissolve any lumps of flour. Heat the mixture, still over medium-low heat, stirring often, until it is bubbling vigorously and has thickened, about 3 minutes. Gradually add the hot stock while stirring gently with a wooden spoon. Heat until a few bubbles break on the surface and then continue to cook, stirring very slowly, for about 3 minutes longer. The mixture should be pale beige and opaque. If the liquid starts to stick to the bottom of the pan, move the pan off the heat, whisk to recombine the ingredients, and let cool slightly.

Add the broccoli purée and seasonings

7 Add the broccoli purée to the milk-stock mixture and stir until blended. Add the salt and pepper, reduce the heat so that small bubbles only occasionally break the surface, cover, and cook for 10 minutes. During this time, uncover the pan once or twice and stir the soup base to make sure it is not sticking to the bottom. Remove the pan from the heat and let the soup base cool to lukewarm.

CHEF'S TIP
If the soup solids are beginning to stick to the pan bottom and burn, pour the soup into a clean saucepan, leaving the burned portion behind, and continue with the recipe. Always taste the soup to be sure it does not have a burned flavor, and discard it and start again if it does.

8 Purée the soup

If you are not sure how to purée in a food processor or blender, turn to page 42. Working in batches to ensure an even consistency, ladle the broccoli mixture into a food processor or blender and purée; take care not to overfill the container as spattering can occur. Stop the machine occasionally to scrape down the sides with a narrow rubber spatula as necessary. Continue to process until the mixture is smooth, then return it to the pan. (I don't recommend using an immersion blender for this step, as it doesn't purée the broccoli smoothly.)

CHEF'S TIP

If you are not serving puréed vegetable soups—particularly green ones—right away, cool them quickly in an ice bath to preserve their color. When ready to serve, reheat them gently and serve right away.

9 Adjust the consistency

Preheat the oven to 200°F (95°C) and place individual bowls in the oven to warm. When all of the soup has been puréed, taste a small spoonful of it. If it doesn't feel perfectly smooth in your mouth, pass it through a medium-mesh sieve placed over a large bowl, pressing against it with the back of a metal or wooden spoon. This step will remove any fibers that were not broken up in the food processor or blender. Don't forget to scrape any purée clinging to the underside of the sieve into the bowl. Pour the soup back into the saucepan and stir in the cream. Place over low heat and reheat gently, stirring constantly, until hot, about 5 minutes. Do not allow it to boil. If the soup seems too thick, thin it with a little milk, adding it ¼ cup (2 fl oz/60 ml) at a time.

10 Adjust the seasonings

Taste the soup. It should taste mainly of fresh broccoli, with an underlying richness and creaminess from the stock and cream. If you feel it tastes bland, stir in additional salt and pepper a little at a time, stirring and tasting after each addition, until the seasonings are to your liking.

11 Serve the soup

Ladle the soup into the warmed bowls. If desired, garnish with the reserved floret pieces. Serve right away.

Finishing touches

In addition to giving your soup a little extra flair with minimal effort, a vegetable garnish gives diners an edible clue as to what they are about to eat. Sautéing the garnishes in butter enhances their flavor and also warms them gently so they don't affect the temperature of the soup when placed on top. This technique works well with cauliflower florets and asparagus tips as well as broccoli florets (see variations, page 98).

Cutting the garnish (top left)
Select ¼ cup (½ oz/15 g) of the smallest unblemished florets to use for garnish. Using scissors, cut the florets into ½-inch (12-mm) pieces and steam them, keeping them slightly separated, with the rest of the broccoli.

Sautéing the garnish (left)
Just before serving the soup, melt 1 teaspoon unsalted butter over low heat. Add the broccoli florets and heat briefly, stirring until warm.

Placing the garnish (above)
After ladling the broccoli soup into warmed mugs or bowls, carefully lay the warm, sautéed florets on the surface of the soup.

Cream Soup Variations

Once you have mastered the skills—making a roux, puréeing the soup, adjusting the consistency with milk—needed to make Cream of Broccoli Soup (page 93), you are ready to make these six variations, each based on one or more popular vegetables. Most of the vegetables can be found year-round, so you won't have to wait for a bowl of earthy Cream of Mushroom Soup or hearty Cream of Vegetable Soup. But some vegetables are best when used during their prime season, such as asparagus spears in spring and early summer and cauliflower during the cool days of fall. Each variation makes 4 to 6 servings.

Cream of Cauliflower Soup

Related to broccoli, cauliflower has a mild but hearty flavor, and its snowy white florets make a smooth ivory soup.

Follow the recipe for Cream of Broccoli Soup, replacing the broccoli with 1 head cauliflower, about 1 lb (500 g). Trim off about ¼ inch (6 mm) from the base, then trim off and discard any leaves. Quarter the trimmed cauliflower head through the stem and then cut it into ½-inch (12-mm) pieces.

Proceed with the recipe starting at step 2, steaming the cauliflower instead of the broccoli. Garnish each bowl of soup with 1 tablespoon snipped fresh chives.

Cream of Asparagus Soup

The vivid color and bright flavor of asparagus shine through in this easy-to-prepare cream soup.

Follow the recipe for Cream of Broccoli Soup, replacing the broccoli with 2 lb (1 kg) asparagus. Bend the stem end of each spear until it breaks naturally and discard the tough ends. Use a vegetable peeler to peel away the thick, fibrous skin from each spear to within about 1 inch (2.5 cm) of the tip. Cut the trimmed asparagus into slices ¼ inch (6 mm) thick.

Proceed with the recipe starting at step 2, steaming the asparagus instead of the broccoli and reducing the steaming time to 3–5 minutes.

Cream of Mushroom Soup

Sautéed mushrooms make a hearty yet refined soup when puréed with milk and stock and garnished with crème fraîche.

Follow the recipe for Cream of Broccoli Soup, replacing the broccoli with 1¼ lb (625 g) chopped fresh cremini mushrooms and ¼ cup (1½ oz/45 g) minced shallots. In a large, heavy frying pan over medium heat, melt 2 tablespoons unsalted butter. Add the mushrooms and shallots and sauté for about 1 minute. Reduce the heat to medium-low, cover, and cook until the mushrooms are soft, about 5 minutes. Uncover, raise the heat to high, and cook, stirring, until the mushroom juices evaporate, about 3 minutes. Do not allow the mushrooms to brown. Stir in 1 teaspoon kosher salt and ⅛ teaspoon freshly ground pepper.

Proceed with the recipe starting at step 3, puréeing the cooked mushroom mixture instead of the broccoli.

Garnish each serving with 1½ teaspoons crème fraîche or heavy (double) cream, swirled in the center.

Cream of Spinach Soup

In France, a pinch of freshly grated nutmeg is the secret ingredient in many spinach dishes. Here, it accents a simple spinach soup.

Follow the recipe for Cream of Broccoli Soup, replacing the broccoli with 3 lb (1.5 kg) spinach. Remove and discard the tough stems. Rinse the leaves in several changes of cool water to remove all sand and grit. Put the spinach, with just the rinsing water clinging to the leaves, in a wide saucepan, place over medium heat, cover, and cook until the leaves are wilted and tender, about 3 minutes. Uncover once or twice and turn the leaves with tongs to ensure even cooking. Transfer the cooked spinach to a sieve placed over a bowl and press on the leaves with the back of a large metal spoon or wide rubber spatula to extract as much water as possible. The spinach should be fairly dry. Put the spinach on a cutting board and use a chef's knife to chop coarsely.

Proceed with the recipe starting at step 3, puréeing the chopped spinach instead of the broccoli. Add ½ teaspoon freshly grated nutmeg to the seasonings.

Garnish each serving with 1½ teaspoons heavy (double) cream, swirled in the center, and a light dusting of nutmeg.

Cream of Onion Soup

Sweet onions, such as Walla Walla, Maui, or Vidalia, deliver a natural sweetness to this silky cream soup.

Follow the recipe for Cream of Broccoli Soup, replacing the broccoli with 1½ lb (750 g) thinly sliced sweet onions. In a large, heavy frying pan over medium heat, melt 2 tablespoons unsalted butter. Add the onions and stir to coat with the butter. Reduce the heat to low, cover, and sauté until softened, about 5 minutes. Uncover and sauté until golden, 10–12 minutes.

Proceed with the recipe starting at step 3, puréeing the cooked onion mixture instead of the broccoli. If necessary, pass the onion purée through a medium-mesh sieve set over a bowl, pressing with the back of a large metal spoon or wide rubber spatula to achieve a perfectly smooth purée.

Just before serving, stir in ½ cup (4 fl oz/ 125 ml) dry sherry, if desired, and heat through.

Cream of Vegetable Soup

All of these ingredients are typically on hand, making this old-fashioned soup a quick-and-easy midweek supper.

Follow the recipe for Cream of Broccoli Soup, replacing the broccoli with 2 cups (10 oz/315 g) peeled and chopped carrots, 2 cups (8 oz/250 g) chopped yellow onion, ½ cup (2½ oz/75 g) chopped celery, and 1 chopped garlic clove. Put the vegetables in a large heavy saucepan with 1 cup (8 fl oz/250 ml) Chicken Stock (page 18) or Vegetable Stock (page 24). Bring to a simmer over medium heat, cover, and cook until the vegetables are tender, about 10 minutes.

Proceed with the recipe starting at step 3, puréeing the mixed vegetable mixture instead of the broccoli.

Garnish each serving with a generous sprinkle of minced fresh flat-leaf (Italian) parsley.

New England Clam Chowder

This creamy version of an American classic is chock-full of fresh clams and chunky potatoes. The broth base is made from steaming the clams, capturing every last drop of the shellfish "liquor." A few slices of crisply fried bacon do double duty, helping to both flavor the soup and provide an appealingly crunchy garnish.

1 **Make the clam broth**
In a wide saucepan over high heat, combine the water, onion slice, celery, bay leaf, garlic clove, and salt and bring to a boil. Reduce the heat to low, cover, and cook for 20 minutes to blend the flavors.

2 **Clean the clams**
While the broth is simmering, clean the clams. To find out more about cleaning clams, turn to page 39. Discard any clams that do not close when gently tapped, then place the rest in a large bowl with cold salted water to cover and let them stand for 10 minutes. Then, rub your fingers over the shells of 1 or 2 clams. If they do not feel gritty, gently drain off the water, rub each clam with a damp kitchen towel, place in a colander, and rinse briefly with water. If they do feel gritty, scrub them with a stiff-bristled brush, following the contours in the shell, then place in a colander and rinse well with water.

3 **Steam the clams in the broth**
Add the clams to the simmering broth. Raise the heat to medium-high, cover the pan, and bring the liquid to a rolling boil. This will take only 1–2 minutes, so don't walk away from the stove. Once the liquid boils, lift the lid and take a peek. Be quick about it—you don't want steam to escape. If the clams have already opened, uncover the pot and remove it from the heat immediately. Littlenecks take 3–4 minutes; larger cherrystones can take 4–5 minutes. Using a slotted spoon, scoop out the opened clams and place them in a large bowl. Leave any unopened clams in the hot liquid, re-cover, and cook for 1–2 minutes longer. If any clam still fails to open, discard it.

4 **Strain the broth**
Set a fine-mesh sieve over a 4-cup (32–fl oz/1-l) glass measuring cup with a spout. Line the sieve with a triple layer of cheesecloth (muslin) that has been dampened and squeezed dry. Ladle the broth through the sieve, leaving any sandy residue behind in the pan. Retrieve any clam meats that fell from their shells and add to the bowl with the other clams. ›

For the clam broth

3 cups (24 fl oz/750 ml) water

1 thick slice yellow onion

½ stalk celery with leaves

1 bay leaf

1 clove garlic, lightly crushed

1 teaspoon kosher salt

3 lb (1.5 kg) cherrystone or littleneck clams

2 or 3 slices thick-cut lightly smoked bacon, cut into ¼-inch (6-mm) dice

2 yellow onions, diced (page 32)

2 stalks celery, diced (page 35)

2 teaspoons minced garlic (page 33)

1¼ lb (625 g) Yukon gold potatoes, peeled and cut into ¼-inch (6-mm) dice

1 teaspoon fresh thyme leaves

1 teaspoon kosher salt

⅛ teaspoon freshly ground pepper

2 cups (16 fl oz/500 ml) half-and-half (half cream)

MAKES 4 SERVINGS

CHEF'S TIP
To firm up bacon to make it easier to dice, place the slices in a single layer on a sheet of aluminum foil and freeze for about 10 minutes. This also works for pancetta, prosciutto, and raw chicken.

5 Remove the clams from their shells

Working over the bowl to capture any juices, pull the clam meats free with your fingers and place in a clean bowl. Reserve 4 or 8 shells for garnish, if desired; discard the rest. Pour any juices left in the first bowl through the sieve, adding them to the cup with the strained broth. You will need 4 cups (32 fl oz/ 1 l) broth. If there is less, add water to make up the difference. Working over the clean bowl, snip the clams into ½-inch (12-mm) pieces with kitchen scissors. Cover the clams and refrigerate until needed.

6 Cook the bacon

Rinse out the pan, wipe it dry, and place it over medium-low heat. Add the bacon and cook until the fat melts, or *renders,* about 5 minutes. Raise the heat to medium and cook, stirring, until the bacon is golden brown, about 3 minutes. Remove the pan from the heat and pour its contents through a small sieve placed over a heatproof bowl. Transfer the bacon to paper towels to drain. Return 2 tablespoons of the bacon fat to the pan and reserve the remainder for another use, or discard it. (Don't pour the bacon fat down the drain, as it can cause clogs.)

7 Sweat the onions, celery, and garlic

Place the pan over medium-low heat and add the onions and celery. Cook in the bacon fat, stirring, until soft, 10–12 minutes. You don't want them to color. (The technique of cooking vegetables slowly without letting them brown is called *sweating.*) Add the garlic and cook for 1 minute to release its aroma.

8 Cook the potatoes

Add the strained broth to the pan with the vegetables and bring to a boil over high heat. Add the potatoes, thyme, salt, and pepper. Reduce the heat to medium, cover, and cook until the potatoes are tender when pierced with the tip of a knife, 10–12 minutes.

9 Finish the chowder

Preheat the oven to 200°F (95°C) and place individual bowls in the oven to warm. Uncover the pan, stir in the half-and-half, and continue to cook until small bubbles just begin to break the surface of the liquid, about 5 minutes. You don't want it to boil because the half-and-half will curdle. Stir in the clams and any juices in the bowl and heat, stirring constantly, until hot. Once again, be careful not to boil the chowder.

10 Adjust the seasonings

Taste the soup; it should taste like briny clams, with accents of the vegetables and herbs used, in a rich, creamy broth. If you feel it tastes dull, stir in a little more salt or pepper, keeping in mind that the bacon used for garnish is also salty, until the ingredients taste nicely balanced.

11 Serve the soup

Ladle the chowder into the warmed bowls, top with 1 or 2 clam shells, if desired, and the bacon, dividing it evenly. Serve right away.

Chowder Variations

Chowders are traditionally thick and chunky seafood soups enriched with cream, with New England Clam Chowder (page 101) being the most famous member of the family. But other chowders are popular, too, including the three variations presented here. Like their New England cousin, they rely on firm, rich-tasting Yukon gold potatoes, crisp-fried bacon, and a trio of aromatic vegetables (carrot, onion, celery) for their flavor and texture. Two of them, the fish and corn chowders, call for the usual cream as well, while the third one, the chicken chowder, relies on a full-bodied stock and buttery Yukon golds for its distinctive character. Each variation makes 4 to 6 servings.

Fish Chowder

Firm, succulent white fish fillet stars in this chowder.

Cut 1½ lb (750 g) skinless cod, halibut, or other flaky white fish fillets into 2-inch (5-cm) chunks; refrigerate until needed.

In a heavy-bottomed saucepan over medium-low heat, cook 3 slices thick-cut lightly smoked bacon pieces (¼-inch/ 6-mm pieces) until brown, about 3 minutes. Transfer the bacon to a plate. Add 1 cup (4 oz/125 g) *each* diced onion, celery, and carrots to the bacon fat and sweat until tender, about 12 minutes. Add 4 cups (32 fl oz/1 l) Fish Stock (page 26) and bring to a boil. Add 1¼ lb (625 g) peeled and diced Yukon gold potatoes, 1 teaspoon salt, ½ teaspoon thyme, and ¼ teaspoon freshly ground pepper, reduce the heat to medium-low, cover, and simmer until the potatoes are tender, 10–12 minutes.

Add the fish pieces, 1 cup (8 fl oz/250 ml) half-and-half (half cream), and ½ teaspoon red hot-pepper sauce. Simmer until the fish is cooked through and starts to flake, 5–6 minutes.

Adjust the seasonings and serve right away, sprinkled with the bacon and oyster crackers.

Corn Chowder

In summer, substitute 1½ lb (750 g) fresh corn kernels for the frozen corn.

In a heavy-bottomed saucepan over medium-low heat, cook 3 slices thick-cut lightly smoked bacon pieces (¼-inch/ 6-mm pieces) until brown, about 3 minutes. Transfer the bacon to a plate. Add 2 diced yellow onions, 2 diced celery stalks, 1 cup (4 oz/125 g) diced carrots, and 2 teaspoons minced garlic to the bacon fat and sweat until tender, about 12 minutes. Add 4 cups (32 fl oz/1 l) Chicken Stock (page 18) and bring to a boil. Add 1¼ lb (625 g) peeled and diced Yukon gold potatoes, 1½ lb (750 g) frozen corn kernels, 1 teaspoon kosher salt, and ¼ teaspoon freshly ground pepper. Reduce the heat to medium-low, cover, and simmer, until the potatoes are tender, 10–12 minutes.

Transfer 3 cups (24 fl oz/750 ml) of the soup to a bowl and let cool slightly, then purée in a food processor or blender. Return the purée to the pan. Add 1 cup (8 fl oz/250 ml) half-and-half (half cream) and ½ teaspoon red hot-pepper sauce and heat through. Adjust the seasonings and serve right away, sprinkled with the bacon.

Chicken Chowder

To save time, buy a roast chicken at your local deli to make this chowder.

Cut 4 cups (24 oz/750 g) cooked chicken meat into 1-inch (2.5-cm) pieces and set aside.

In a heavy-bottomed saucepan over medium-low heat, cook 3 slices thick-cut lightly smoked bacon pieces (¼-inch/ 6-mm pieces) until brown, about 3 minutes. Transfer the bacon to a plate. Add 2 tablespoons unsalted butter to the bacon fat. Add 2 diced yellow onions, 2 diced celery stalks, 1 cup (4 oz/125 g) diced carrots, 2 teaspoons minced garlic, and 1 small seeded and diced red bell pepper (capsicum) and sweat until tender, about 12 minutes. Add 3 cups (24 fl oz/ 750 ml) Chicken Stock (page 18) and bring to a boil. Add 1¼ lb (625 g) peeled and diced Yukon gold potatoes, ¼ teaspoon red hot-pepper sauce, 1 teaspoon salt, and ⅛ teaspoon freshly ground pepper, reduce the heat to medium-low, cover, and simmer until the potatoes are tender, 10–12 minutes.

Add the chicken pieces and stir constantly until heated through. Adjust the seasonings and serve right away, sprinkled with the bacon.

Shrimp Bisque

This traditional bisque, with the consistency of the finest cream soup, gets its thick velvety texture from puréed cooked shrimp, heavy cream, and cooked white rice. Its delicate rust color comes from the addition of tomato paste, and the deep taste of the sea is the result of a carefully made shellfish stock.

1 **Prepare the shells for the stock**
If you need help making shellfish stock, turn to page 28. Using a large, heavy knife, chop the shrimp shells into small (about 1-inch/2.5-cm) pieces. Put the lobster or crab shells, if using, in a heavy-duty locking plastic bag and, using a rolling pin or meat pounder, break them into small pieces.

2 **Simmer the stock**
Place all the shells in an 8-qt (8-l) heavy-bottomed pot. Add water to cover the shells by 1 inch (2.5 cm) and place the pot on the stove top over medium-high heat. Without stirring, slowly bring the liquid to a boil. As soon as you see large bubbles begin to form, reduce the heat until only small bubbles occasionally break the surface of the liquid. Use a large slotted spoon to skim the grayish foam that rises to the surface. Never stir the stock, which will make it cloudy. Put the parsley, thyme, and bay leaf in a large square of dampened cheesecloth (muslin), secure it with kitchen string, and add it to the pot. Add the wine, onion, carrot, celery, tomato paste, and peppercorns. Adjust the heat to maintain a gentle simmer and cook, uncovered, until the liquid has a good shellfish flavor, about 30 minutes. Stir in the salt and remove the pot from the heat.

3 **Strain the stock**
Line a sieve with a triple layer of damp cheesecloth and place it over a large bowl. Set the bowl in the sink, if you like, to make cleanup easier. Ladle or carefully pour the stock through the sieve. Discard the solids in the sieve and let the stock cool to lukewarm. Measure out 3 cups (24 fl oz/750 ml) to use for the bisque. Cover and refrigerate the remaining stock for up to 2 days or freeze for up to 2 months.

4 **Peel and devein the shrimp**
If you are not sure how to peel and devein shrimp, turn to page 38. Peel and devein the shrimp, separating the meat from the shells and the heads, if they are attached. Coarsely chop the shrimp meat, cover, and refrigerate. You can freeze the leftover shells for a future use or discard. ❯

For the shellfish stock

4 cups (1½ lb/750 g) mixed shells from shrimp (prawns), preferably with the heads intact, lobster, or crab

2 sprigs fresh flat-leaf (Italian) parsley

1 sprig fresh thyme

1 bay leaf

½ cup (4 fl oz/125 ml) dry white wine such as Sauvignon Blanc

1 large yellow onion, cut into thick slices

1 carrot, peeled and cut on the diagonal into slices ½ inch (12 mm) thick

1 stalk celery, cut on the diagonal into slices ½ inch (12 mm) thick

2 tablespoons tomato paste

8–10 whole peppercorns

1 tablespoon kosher salt

1 lb (500 g) uncooked shrimp (prawns) in the shell, preferably with heads intact

2 tablespoons unsalted butter

¼ cup (1 oz/30 g) chopped shallots

½ cup (4 fl oz/125 ml) dry white wine such as Sauvignon Blanc

3 tablespoons raw long-grain white rice

1 tablespoon tomato paste

1 cup (8 fl oz/250 ml) heavy (double) cream

½ teaspoon kosher salt

⅛ teaspoon cayenne pepper, plus a sprinkle for garnish, optional

¼ cup (2 fl oz/60 ml) dry sherry or Madeira, optional

MAKES 4–6 SERVINGS

5 Make the bisque base
Place a large saucepan over medium-low heat and add the butter. When the butter melts and the foam begins to subside, add the shallots and cook, stirring, until softened, about 5 minutes. Raise the heat to medium, stir in the wine, and heat until large bubbles form on the surface of the liquid. Add the reserved 3 cups stock, the rice, and tomato paste and return to a boil. Reduce the heat until only small bubbles occasionally break the surface of the liquid, cover the pan, and simmer until the rice is soft, 20–25 minutes.

6 Add the shrimp to the bisque base
Uncover the pan, add the reserved chopped shrimp, and cook, stirring, until the shrimp turn from translucent to opaque. Don't walk away from the stove, as this will take only about 2 minutes. Remove the pan from the heat and let the mixture cool to lukewarm.

7 Purée the bisque
If you are not sure how to purée in a blender, turn to page 42. Working in batches to ensure an even consistency, ladle the soup into a blender and process to a smooth purée. Take care not to overfill the blender, as spattering can occur. (A blender is best for this step because it aerates the bisque, giving it a very smooth and creamy texture.) Start blending at the lowest speed and gradually increase it. Keep your hand on the lid, as steam from the hot liquids can force it off. Stop the blender occasionally to scrape down the sides with a narrow rubber spatula as necessary. Pour the purée back into the pan.

8 Finish the bisque
Preheat the oven to 200°F (95°C) and place individual bowls in the oven to warm. Return the pan to the lowest possible setting. Add the cream, salt, and ⅛ teaspoon cayenne pepper, whisking very slowly until the ingredients are blended. Then add the sherry, if using, and again whisk very slowly until the ingredients are blended. You do not want the bisque to boil, so reheat the soup gently, stirring every now and again, until it is hot, about 5 minutes.

9 Adjust the seasonings
Taste the soup; it should taste primarily of shrimp with an underlying richness from the stock, puréed rice, and cream. The optional sherry will add an interesting nutty counterpoint. If you feel the soup tastes dull, stir in a little more salt, cayenne, or sherry until the flavors are nicely balanced.

10 Serve the bisque
Ladle the soup into the warmed bowls, sprinkle with a small amount of cayenne, if desired, and serve right away.

Bisque Variations

The classic bisque is a puréed shellfish soup—shrimp, lobster, crab, and crayfish are the most common types—made by first preparing a stock from the crushed shells and then thickening the base with rice or bread. Nowadays, the term has been expanded to embrace creamy puréed vegetable soups made with other stocks, such as the Tomato Bisque included here. When making any of the following variations, however, the basic lessons you learned making Shrimp Bisque (page 105) apply: start by making a full-flavored stock, thicken the base with a little rice, and finally, purée the bisque until perfectly smooth. Each variation makes 4 to 6 servings.

Lobster or Crab Bisque

This intensely flavored rich soup is often served in a small, round soup dish called a bisque cup.

In a large saucepan over medium-low heat, melt 2 tablespoons unsalted butter. Add ¼ cup (1 oz/30 g) chopped shallots and sauté until softened, about 5 minutes. Raise the heat to medium, stir in ½ cup (4 fl oz/125 ml) dry white wine, and bring to a boil. Add 2 cups (16 fl oz/500 ml) Shellfish Stock (page 28), 1 cup (8 fl oz/250 ml) Beef Stock (page 20), 3 tablespoons raw long-grain white rice, and 1 tablespoon tomato paste and return to a boil. Reduce the heat to low, cover, and simmer until the rice is soft, 20–25 minutes.

Have ready ¾ lb (375 g) cooked lobster meat or crabmeat. Add ½ lb (8 oz/250 g) of the lobster or crabmeat to the pan and let cool to lukewarm. Purée until smooth, then pour back into the pan. Stir in 1 cup (8 fl oz/250 ml) heavy (double) cream, ½ teaspoon kosher salt, and ⅛ teaspoon cayenne pepper and reheat gently. Serve right away, garnished with the reserved lobster or crabmeat.

Mussel Bisque

A few drops of hot-pepper sauce heighten the brininess of the mussels.

In a large saucepan, bring 3 cups (24 fl oz/750 ml) Fish Stock (page 26) to a boil. Add 3 lb (1.5 kg) well-scrubbed mussels, cover, and cook until the shells open, 2–3 minutes. Set aside the opened mussels, discard any unopened ones, and strain the stock through a fine-mesh sieve lined with cheesecloth (muslin).

In a large saucepan over medium-low heat, melt 2 tablespoons unsalted butter. Add ¼ cup (1 oz/30 g) chopped shallots and sauté until softened. Raise the heat to medium, stir in ½ cup (4 fl oz/125 ml) dry white wine, and bring to a boil. Add the strained stock, 3 tablespoons raw long-grain white rice, and 1 tablespoon tomato paste and return to a boil. Reduce the heat to low, cover, and simmer until the rice is soft, 20–25 minutes.

Remove the mussels from their shells. Set aside one-third of the meats; add the rest to the pan and let cool to lukewarm. Purée until smooth, then pour back into the pan. Stir in 1 cup (8 fl oz/250 ml) heavy (double) cream, ½ teaspoon kosher salt, and 3 drops red hot-pepper sauce and reheat gently. Serve right away, garnished with the reserved mussels.

Tomato Bisque

A generous addition of cream turns this nontraditional bisque a warm, deep pink.

In a large saucepan over medium-low heat, melt 2 tablespoons unsalted butter. Add ⅓ cup (1½ oz/45 g) chopped shallots and 2 minced garlic cloves and cook, stirring, until softened, about 3 minutes. Add 2½ cups (20 fl oz/625 ml) Vegetable Stock (page 24), 3 tablespoons raw long-grain white rice, and ½ teaspoon kosher salt and bring to a boil. Reduce the heat to low, cover, and cook until the rice is soft, 20–25 minutes.

Add 1 can (28 oz/875 g) crushed plum (Roma) tomatoes with juice and 1 tablespoon torn fresh basil leaves. Cover and simmer for 10 minutes. Let the mixture cool to lukewarm. Purée until smooth, then push the mixture through a sieve with the back of a ladle and return to the saucepan over low heat. Whisk in 1 cup (8 fl oz/250 ml) heavy (double) cream, ¼ teaspoon kosher salt, ⅛ teaspoon white pepper, and 3 drops red hot-pepper sauce and reheat gently. Adjust the seasonings. Serve right away, garnished with small croutons.

Cheddar Cheese Soup

Simple and hearty, this old-fashioned soup is a sunny yellow from the deeply colored Cheddar cheese that makes up its base. Dry mustard and hot-pepper sauce both provide a welcome touch of warm spice to the rich, smooth soup, while a garnish of white Cheddar adds pleasing visual contrast.

2 cups (16 fl oz/500 ml) whole milk

2 cups (16 fl oz/500 ml) Chicken Stock (page 18)

4 tablespoons (2 oz/60 g) unsalted butter

¼ cup (1½ oz/45 g) grated yellow onion

¼ cup (1½ oz/45 g) all-purpose (plain) flour

½ lb (250 g) sharp yellow Cheddar cheese, coarsely shredded

1 teaspoon kosher salt

1 teaspoon dry mustard

¼ teaspoon red hot-pepper sauce

½ cup (2 oz/60 g) finely shredded sharp white Cheddar cheese

MAKES 4 SERVINGS

CHEF'S TIP

For the best results when cooking with cheese, do not use reduced-fat or fat-free cheeses, unless the recipe specifically states they are acceptable. These types of cheese are made by a different process than true cheese and using them will affect the flavor and texture of a recipe.

1 **Heat the liquids**
Pour the milk and stock into separate small saucepans and place them over low heat. Heat the milk and stock just until small bubbles form around the edge of the pan, then remove them from the heat. Do not let the liquids boil.

2 **Make the roux**
If you are not sure how to make a roux, turn to page 40 (this recipe incorporates onion into the roux). Place a heavy-bottomed saucepan over medium-low heat and add the butter. When the butter has melted and the foam begins to subside, add the onion and cook, stirring, for 1 minute to soften. Sprinkle the flour evenly over the butter and onion. Stir with a wooden spoon or heatproof spatula until the flour is completely blended with the butter and no lumps of flour are visible, about 2 minutes.

3 **Add the liquids to the roux**
Gradually add the hot milk to the pan with the onion roux while stirring gently with a small whisk to dissolve any lumps of flour. Heat the mixture, still over medium-low heat, stirring often, until the mixture thickens to the consistency of very thick cream, about 3 minutes longer. Gradually add the hot stock while stirring gently. Heat the mixture until a few small bubbles break the surface and then continue to cook, stirring very slowly, about 3 minutes longer. The mixture will be light beige. Reduce the heat to the lowest level.

4 **Finish the soup**
Preheat the oven to 200°F (95°C) and place individual bowls in the oven to warm. Add the yellow Cheddar cheese, salt, dry mustard, and hot-pepper sauce and stir until the cheese is almost melted. Do not let the mixture boil at this point, or the cheese will separate and the soup will be grainy.

5 **Adjust the seasonings and serve the soup**
Taste the soup; it should taste of pleasantly tangy cheese with just a hint of spice. If you feel tastes bland, stir in additional salt, dry mustard, or hot-pepper sauce a little at a time, stirring and tasting after each addition, until the flavor is to your liking. Ladle the soup into the warmed bowls and garnish each bowl with 2 tablespoons of finely shredded white Cheddar cheese. Serve right away.

6

Stews

Stews are similar to soups but are generally more substantial. Indeed, the recipes in this chapter are so loaded with meat or seafood and vegetables that they make ideal one-pot meals. The skills you have mastered making soups in the previous chapters—how to simmer a stock, how to cook a roux, how to purée vegetables—can now be used to make a variety of popular and regional stews.

1

3

4

5

MASTER RECIPE

Chicken, Shrimp & Andouille Gumbo

A nutty, slowly cooked brown roux adds a distinctive flavor to this stew, which boasts chunks of sweet shrimp, meaty poached chicken, and spicy andouille sausage in a complex, but not-too-thick broth. Okra, a traditional gumbo ingredient, lends fresh flavor and natural thickening power to the stew.

1 Poach the chicken

Rinse the chicken with cold water and drain. In a large, heavy-bottomed pot, combine the chicken, sliced celery, bay leaf, salt, and cayenne. Add the 2½ qt (2½ l) water, place over medium-high heat, and bring to a boil. As soon as you see large bubbles begin to form, reduce the heat until only small bubbles occasionally break the surface. Use a large spoon to skim off any foam that rises to the surface as the water comes to a boil. Cover the pot and cook the chicken until pieces separate easily from the rest of the carcass when pulled or prodded with tongs or a large spoon, about 1 hour.

2 Strain the broth

Using a slotted spoon and tongs, carefully lift the chicken out of the pot and place it on a platter; don't worry if the chicken breaks apart. Line a sieve with a triple layer of dampened cheesecloth (muslin) and place over a large bowl. Ladle the broth through the sieve. Discard the solids. Use a large spoon to skim the fat off the surface of the broth and discard the fat. Measure out 5 cups (40 fl oz/1.25 l) of the broth; set the remaining broth aside.

3 Shred the chicken

When the chicken is cool enough to handle, remove the skin and discard. With your fingers, pull the chicken from the bones and shred the meat into large pieces. Put the chicken pieces in a bowl and set aside.

4 Prepare the onion, bell pepper, celery, and garlic

For more details on working with these vegetables, turn to pages 32–36. First, dice the onion: Cut the onion in half lengthwise and peel each half. Place each half, cut side down, on the cutting board. Make a series of lengthwise cuts, then a series of parallel cuts, and lastly cut crosswise to create ¼-inch (6-mm) dice. Then, dice the bell pepper: Halve the pepper and pull out the stems, seeds, and ribs. Cut each half into strips ¼ inch wide, line up the strips, and then cut crosswise into ¼-inch dice. Next, cut the celery into ¼-inch dice. Finally, mince the garlic: Place the cloves on a work surface, firmly press against them with the flat side of a knife, and pull away the papery skin. Mince the garlic.

5 Prepare the okra

Trim off the tops of the okra, if present, and discard. Cut each piece of okra crosswise into slices ½ inch (12 mm) thick.

For the poached chicken

1 whole chicken, about 3 lb (1.5 kg)

1 stalk celery, sliced

1 bay leaf

1½ teaspoons kosher salt

½ teaspoon cayenne pepper

2½ qt (2½ l) water

1 yellow onion

½ green bell pepper (capsicum)

1 stalk celery

2 cloves garlic

1 lb (500 g) fresh okra

½ lb (250 g) small or medium shrimp (prawns) in the shell, preferably with heads intact

1 tablespoon canola oil, plus ½ cup (4 fl oz/125 ml)

5½ cups (44 fl oz/1.35 l) water

½ cup (2½ oz/75 g) all-purpose (plain) flour

¾ lb (375 g) andouille sausage

2 cups (14 oz/440 g) long-grain white rice

½ teaspoon kosher salt

⅛ teaspoon freshly ground black pepper

MAKES 6–8 SERVINGS

MAKE-AHEAD TIP

Poach and shred the chicken up to 1 day before you plan to serve the soup. Cool the broth over an ice bath, then cover and refrigerate with the chicken.

Cutting the spicy andouille into slices as well as into cubes provides a diversity of texture in the gumbo, which enhances the flavor and overall appearance of the finished stew.

6 **Peel and devein the shrimp**
If you are not sure how to peel and devein shrimp, turn to page 38. Peel each shrimp, first pulling off the head, if still attached, followed by the legs on the inside curve of the shell. Then, starting at the head end, carefully pull away the shell from the meat. Rinse and reserve the shells. Using a paring knife, make a shallow groove down the back of each shrimp and lift out the dark veinlike digestive tract with the tip of the knife. (If you are using small shrimp and the vein is not visible, skip the deveining step.) Place the cleaned shrimp in a bowl, cover, and refrigerate until ready to cook.

7 **Make the shrimp broth**
Heat a large saucepan over medium-high heat until hot enough to make a drop of water sizzle on contact. Pour the 1 tablespoon canola oil into the pan. Add the shrimp shells, raise the heat to high, and cook, stirring, until the shells are dark red and somewhat browned, about 5 minutes. Add 2 cups (16 fl oz/500 ml) of the water, bring to a boil, reduce the heat to medium-low, and cook until the broth has a good shrimp flavor, 2–3 minutes. Remove the pan from the heat and let the mixture cool to lukewarm. Transfer the shells and cooking water to a food processor and process until the shells are coarsely chopped. Pour the contents of the processor into a fine-mesh sieve placed over a large glass measuring cup or bowl and, using the back of a large spoon, press down hard on the shells to extract as much flavor as possible. Discard the solids in the sieve. Cover the broth and refrigerate until needed.

8 **Make the roux**
In a heavy-bottomed frying pan, combine the ½ cup canola oil and sprinkle the flour evenly over the oil. Stir with a wooden spoon until the flour is completely blended with the oil and no lumps of flour are visible, about 2 minutes. Place over medium heat and cook the roux, stirring constantly, until it turns a rich, dark brown. This will take about 20 minutes, so be patient. As the roux cooks, adjust the heat as needed to keep the mixture bubbling gently. For more information on how to make a brown roux, turn to page 40.

9 **Cook the gumbo base**
Cut half the andouille into cubes and set it aside. Cut the remaining andouille into slices ¼ inch (6 mm) thick. Place a large, heavy-bottomed pot over medium-low heat, add all of the andouille, the onion, bell pepper, celery, and garlic and cook, stirring, until the vegetables have softened, about 8 minutes. Add the roux, using a heatproof spatula to scrape every bit into the pot, and stir to coat the vegetables well with the roux. Add the reserved shrimp broth and the 5 cups (40 fl oz/1.25 l) chicken broth, raise the heat to medium-high, and bring to a boil. As soon as you see large bubbles begin to form, reduce the heat until only small bubbles occasionally break the surface of the liquid. Cover the pan partially and simmer for about 1 hour. The gumbo base will be lightly thickened and fragrant.

10 Cook the rice
Pour the rice into a saucepan with a tight-fitting lid. Add the remaining 3½ cups (28 fl oz/875 ml) water and the salt. Place over high heat and heat until large bubbles form on the surface of the water. Stir the rice with a wooden spoon, cover the pan, and reduce the heat to low. Cook until the rice has absorbed all of the water and is tender when you bite into it, 15–20 minutes. Uncover the pan, fluff the kernels with a fork, and let the rice stand until serving time.

11 Cook the okra and shrimp
Preheat the oven to 200°F (95°F) and place individual bowls in the oven to warm. Increase the heat under the gumbo base to medium-low, add the chicken meat, and cook, stirring, for 1 minute. Add the okra and cook, stirring, until it is almost tender, about 6 minutes. Stir in the shrimp and cook just until they turn from translucent to opaque, about 3 minutes.

12 Finish the gumbo
The gumbo should be quite soupy, not thick like most stews. If it is too thick, thin it with the remaining chicken broth, adding it ¼ cup (2 fl oz/60 ml) at a time until the desired consistency is reached.

13 Adjust the seasonings
Add the black pepper and taste the gumbo; it should be rich from the chicken, sweet from the shrimp, and somewhat spicy from the andouille, with no single flavor dominating. If you feel it tastes dull, stir in a little more salt or black pepper until the flavors are nicely balanced. Keep in mind that the rice will mellow the flavors somewhat.

14 Serve the gumbo
Spoon the gumbo into the warmed bowls and divide the rice evenly among all the bowls. Serve right away.

CHEF'S TIP
Giant and jumbo shrimp are often called prawns, although true prawns are actually either certain small members of the lobster family, or crustaceans that spawn in freshwater. They look like shrimp, but have more elongated bodies.

Finishing touches

Gumbo is traditionally served with a carefully rounded scoop of white rice to soak up the juices, but the presentation can be dressed up a bit by drawing on ingredients from the recipe and using them to create a variety of garnishes. Keeping a shellfish whole and in its shell for garnish is a trick used by restaurant chefs all over the world. Green onions bring out the green of the okra, while lemons brighten the shrimp.

Whole shrimp (top left)

Steam a whole shrimp (prawn) with the head still on for about 3 minutes and perch it on top of each bowl of gumbo to make a dramatic—and edible—statement.

Green onions (left)

Thinly slice on the diagonal the green parts of 2 or 3 green (spring) onions and distribute the slices among the bowls. Choose a few perfect examples of the slightly curled ends and toss those in as well.

Lemon slices (above)

While not used in the recipe, a squirt or two of fresh lemon juice perks up the flavors of any soup, especially one with seafood. Garnish bowls with lemon slices for additional color and flavor.

Bouillabaisse

MASTER RECIPE

In this adaptation of the familiar Provençal fish stew, a tomato-based broth, richly scented with fennel, herbs, and saffron, flavors sea-fresh fish. A spoonful of *rouille*, a thick, spicy, rust-hued sauce, adds color and flavor to each serving, while toasted baguette slices, placed in the bowls, give the stew body.

1 Prepare the bell pepper and potato for the *rouille*

Using tongs, hold the bell pepper over the flame of a gas stove until the skin is blackened on all sides. (Alternatively, char the skin under a broiler/grill.) Transfer the pepper to a paper bag, let cool, then scrape off the blackened skin with a paring knife. Use a chef's knife to cut off the top, remove the seeds and ribs, then cut the pepper into rough pieces. Measure out ½ cup (3 oz/90 g) pepper pieces and reserve the rest for another use. Cut the peeled potatoes into ½-inch (12-mm) dice and place the pieces in a saucepan. Add water to cover by 1 inch (2.5 cm) and bring to a boil over high heat. Reduce the heat to medium and cook until the potatoes are tender when pierced with the tip of a knife, 10–15 minutes. Measure out 1 cup (5 oz/155 g) cooked potatoes and reserve the remainder for another use.

2 Make the *rouille*

In a food processor, combine the ½ cup bell pepper, ½ cup potatoes, the garlic, salt, and red pepper flakes and process until smooth. With the motor running, slowly add the olive oil in a thin, steady stream until incorporated. Transfer the *rouille* to a bowl, cover, and refrigerate until needed.

3 Prepare the vegetables and orange zest

First, slice the fennel: Trim off the stems and feathery tops of the fennel bulb, if still attached. Save some of the feathery tops for garnish. Pull off and discard the outer layer of the bulb if it is bruised or tough. Cut the bulb in half lengthwise, then thinly cut the fennel crosswise into half-moons. Then, slice the onion: Cut the onion in half lengthwise and peel each half. Place each half, cut side down, on the cutting board, and cut thin vertical slices from stem to blossom end at ⅛-inch (3-mm) intervals. Next, peel the garlic: Lightly crush the garlic cloves with the flat side of a chef's knife and peel but do not mince or chop. Finally, zest the orange: Scrub the orange to remove any traces of wax, then use a paring knife to peel off 2 strips of orange zest. Each strip should be 2 inches (5 cm) long and ½ inch (12 mm) wide. Make sure you remove only the colored portion of the peel, leaving the bitter white pith behind. Reserve the orange for another use.

4 Make the broth

Place a heavy-bottomed pot over medium-low heat and add the olive oil. When the oil appears to shimmer, add the fennel, onion, and garlic. Reduce the heat to low and cook, stirring, until softened, about 10 minutes. Stir in the tomatoes with their juices, the orange zest strips, saffron, basil, parsley, thyme, and fennel seeds.

For the *rouille*

1 red bell pepper (capsicum)

2 large red potatoes, peeled

4 cloves garlic, finely chopped

1 teaspoon kosher salt

½ teaspoon red pepper flakes

½ cup (4 fl oz/125 ml) extra-virgin olive oil

1 small fennel bulb

1 large sweet onion, such as Vidalia or Maui

4 cloves garlic

1 orange

½ cup (4 fl oz/125 ml) extra-virgin olive oil

1 can (28 oz/875 g) diced plum (Roma) tomatoes

2 generous pinches saffron threads

1 sprig fresh basil

1 sprig fresh flat-leaf (Italian) parsley

1 teaspoon fresh thyme leaves

1 teaspoon fennel seeds

6 cups (48 fl oz/1.5 l) Shellfish Stock (page 28)

1 sweet baguette

2 teaspoons kosher salt

¼ teaspoon freshly ground black pepper

2½ lb (1.25 kg) firm, non-oily white fish fillets such as cod, halibut, or snapper, or a combination

¾ lb (375 g) large shrimp (prawns) in the shell

1 lb (500 g) cherrystone or littleneck clams

1 lb (500 g) pound mussels

MAKES 6–8 SERVINGS

5 Simmer the soup base

Raise the heat to high, pour in the stock, and bring to a boil. As soon as you see large bubbles begin to form, reduce the heat until only small bubbles occasionally break the surface of the liquid. Cover the pot and simmer the mixture gently for 45 minutes to create a flavorful broth. Remove the pot from the heat and let the base cool slightly. Measure out 3 tablespoons of the base and set aside.

6 Prepare the bread

While the broth simmers, preheat the oven to 350°F (180°C). Cut the baguette on the diagonal into 16 slices, each 1 inch (2.5 cm) thick. Arrange the bread slices on a rimmed baking sheet, place in the oven, and toast until golden, about 20 minutes. Remove the toasts from the oven and reserve.

7 Pass the soup base through a food mill

For more details on using a food mill, turn to page 43. Fit a food mill with the medium disk and place over a large bowl. Ladle the soup base, including the solids, into the mill and turn the crank to force the mixture through. This process will extract as much flavor from the solids as possible. Discard the solids in the mill. Return the broth to the pot and add the salt and black pepper.

8 Prepare the fish, shrimp, and mollusks

Rinse the fish fillets well and pat dry with paper towels. Cut the fish into 2-inch (5-cm) pieces and set aside. Next, peel the shrimp by first pulling off the heads, if still attached, followed by the legs on the inside curve of the shell. Starting at the head end, carefully pull the shell from the meat. Reserve the shells. Using a small knife, make a shallow cut down the back of each shrimp. Lift out the dark veinlike intestinal tract with the knife's tip. Rinse the shrimp and set aside. Finally, rinse the clams and mussels well, discarding any open ones that do not close when gently tapped. Scrub with a stiff-bristled brush, or wipe with a damp kitchen towel. Pull or scrape away any "beards" from the mussels. Rinse the shells and set aside. For more details on handling shellfish, turn to pages 38–39.

CHEF'S TIP

Unlike most types of stew, shellfish stews don't keep well. For the best flavor and texture, eat them just after cooking.

9 Adjust the consistency of the *rouille*

Remove the bowl of *rouille* from the refrigerator and whisk in the reserved 3 tablespoons bouillabaisse broth until fully combined; it should have the consistency of loose mayonnaise. Let the *rouille* stand until it comes to room temperature, about 30 minutes.

10»

CHEF'S TIP

When making seafood or fish stews, be extra vigilant that the cooking liquid never comes to a boil. The harsh heat can cause the the fish, shrimp, and mollusks to toughen.

10 Cook the seafood

Preheat the oven to 200°F (95°C) and place shallow individual bowls in the oven to warm. Place the broth over medium-high heat and bring to a boil. Add the thicker pieces of fish, reduce the heat to medium, cover, and cook for 5 minutes. Next, add the clams and mussels, the thinner pieces of fish, and the shrimp. Re-cover the pot and cook for about 3 minutes longer. At this point the fish pieces and the shrimp should be just opaque throughout and the clams and mussels should be open; take care not to overcook or boil the stew or the seafood will become tough.

11 Double-check the shellfish

Use a large metal spoon to stir the soup and check all the clams and mussels. If any of the clams or mussels are still closed, use tongs to remove them and discard them.

12 Adjust the seasonings

Taste the soup. If it tastes bland, stir in more salt or black pepper, a pinch at a time. Stir, then taste again and adjust until the seasonings are to your liking.

13 Serve the stew

Place 1 or 2 pieces of toasted bread in the bottom of each warmed bowl. Ladle the broth and seafood over the bread. Garnish with small sprigs of the feathery fennel tops. Serve right away, passing the *rouille* and any extra bread at the table for spooning on the top.

Serving ideas

You can serve the Bouillabaisse one of two ways: For a family gathering, serve the dish as they do in Provence, with the broth course separate from the fish course. For a more formal get-together, ladle the broth and fish into individual bowls, with the bread and rouille either in the bottom of the bowl or on the side. Reserve a few attractive feathery tops of the fennel bulbs and use them as a colorful and flavorful garnish.

Individual serving (top left)
Top the toasted bread with the *rouille* and place it in an empty bowl. Ladle the bouillabaisse over the bread and allow all the flavors to mingle.

Traditional family style (left)
In the south of France, the bouillabaisse broth is typically strained and served as a first course with the *rouille*-smeared croutons alongside. The cooked shrimp (prawns), fish, and mussels are then served as a second course.

Bread on the side (above)
Divide the soup among warmed bowls, place the bowls on a liner plate, and serve with a *rouille*-smeared crouton for dipping.

Beef & Red Wine Stew

Much of the beef sold today is quite lean. It is better for us, but it is also less juicy and tender. Here, a full-bodied red wine helps tenderize the meat to a soft, almost melting texture, while giving the dish a particularly fragrant, rich flavor. The savory root vegetables and earthy mushrooms are perfect complements.

2 slices thick-cut lightly smoked bacon, diced

2 lb (1 kg) well-marbled boneless beef chuck, fat trimmed, cut into 1½-inch (4-cm) pieces and patted dry

1½ teaspoons kosher salt

¼ teaspoon freshly ground pepper

2–3 tablespoons extra-virgin olive oil

1 yellow onion, diced (page 32)

1 carrot or parsnip, peeled and sliced

1 clove garlic, minced (page 33)

2 tablespoons all-purpose (plain) flour

3 cups (24 fl oz/750 ml) Pinot Noir, plus a little more to supplement the liquid

1 bay leaf

1 teaspoon fresh thyme leaves

¾ lb (375 g) small white or brown mushrooms

2 tablespoons finely chopped fresh flat-leaf (Italian) parsley

MAKES 4–6 SERVINGS

CHEF'S TIP
When cooking with wine, use only wine that is good enough to drink by itself. Better yet, use the same wine in the recipe and at the table.

1 **Cook the bacon and brown the beef**
Place a Dutch oven over medium-low heat and add the bacon. Cook, stirring occasionally, until golden, about 10 minutes. Using a slotted spoon, transfer the bacon to a large bowl. Sprinkle the beef pieces evenly with ½ teaspoon of the salt and ⅛ teaspoon of the pepper. Working in batches, add the beef to the pot with the bacon fat and cook over medium heat, stirring occasionally, until browned on all sides, about 10 minutes per batch. As each batch is browned, use the slotted spoon to transfer it to the bowl holding the bacon. If the pot seems dry, add a tablespoon of olive oil. For more details about browning meat, turn to page 41.

2 **Cook the vegetables and oven-braise the stew**
Preheat the oven to 350°F (180°C). Add the onion, carrot, and garlic to the pot, reduce the heat to medium-low, and cook, stirring, until the vegetables are softened, about 5 minutes. Sprinkle the flour evenly over the vegetables and cook, stirring, for about 1 minute until well blended; the flour will help thicken the stew as it cooks. Gradually pour in the wine, stirring constantly. Bring to a boil, scraping up any browned bits on the bottom of the pot. Add the beef, bacon, and any meat juices in the bowl, the bay leaf, thyme, ½ teaspoon of the salt, and the remaining ⅛ teaspoon pepper and stir to blend. Cover the pot, place it in the oven, and cook until the meat is very tender, about 1 hour.

3 **Cook the mushrooms and finish the stew**
Place a large frying pan over medium-high heat and add the remaining 2 tablespoons olive oil. When the oil appears to shimmer, add the mushrooms and cook, stirring, for 1 minute. Cover the pot, reduce the heat to medium-low, and cook until the mushrooms are softened, about 5 minutes. Uncover, raise the heat to high, sprinkle with the remaining ½ teaspoon salt, and cook, stirring, until the liquid has evaporated and the mushrooms are brown, about 5 minutes. Stir the mushrooms into the stew. Re-cover and continue to cook the stew until the beef is very tender when pierced with the tip of a knife, 20–30 minutes. Check periodically to make sure the meat is covered by the liquid and add more wine, ½ cup (4 fl oz/125 ml) at a time, if needed.

4 **Adjust the seasonings and serve the stew**
Remove from the oven, turn off the oven, and let the stew stand, covered, for about 10 minutes. When the oven has cooled slightly, place individual shallow bowls inside to warm. Then, taste the stew; if you feel it tastes dull, stir in a little more salt or pepper until the flavors are nicely balanced. Spoon the stew into the warmed bowls and top with the parsley, dividing evenly. Serve right away.

Irish Lamb Stew

This popular stew does not usually call for carrots, but I like the color and sweetness they add to the overall dish. The potatoes are cut two ways: the smaller pieces break down and help thicken the juices released by the lamb, and the larger ones remain whole, providing substantial texture. Use meaty lamb neck bones, if possible, as they yield the most flavorful result.

1 Prepare the potatoes
Preheat the oven to 350°F (180°C) and peel the potatoes. Cut half of the potatoes into slices ⅛ inch (3 mm) thick. Cut the remaining potatoes into 1-inch (2.5-cm) chunks. Place the potato chunks in a bowl, add water to cover to prevent them from discoloring, and set them aside.

2 Layer the stew ingredients
Spread the sliced potatoes in the bottom of a large Dutch oven or other heavy-bottomed pot. Sprinkle the potato slices with ½ teaspoon of the salt, a pinch of the pepper, and 1 teaspoon of the thyme. Spread the onions on top of the sliced potatoes and sprinkle with ½ teaspoon of the salt, a pinch of the pepper, and 1 teaspoon of the thyme. Top with the carrots, spreading them in an even layer, and then add the lamb in a single layer. Sprinkle the lamb with the remaining 1 teaspoon salt and pinch of pepper. Drain the potato chunks and arrange them in a single layer on top of the meat. Sprinkle with the remaining 1 teaspoon thyme.

3 Oven-braise the stew
Pour the boiling water evenly over the layered stew ingredients. Cover the pot, place on the center rack of the oven, and cook until the lamb, onions, and potatoes are tender when pierced with a fork, about 2 hours. Remove from the oven and let stand, covered, for 10 minutes.

4 Adjust the seasonings
When the oven has cooled slightly, place individual bowls inside to warm. Uncover the stew and stir gently to combine the ingredients. The thinly sliced potatoes will break apart and thicken the lamb juices. Then, taste the stew. If you feel it tastes a little dull, add additional salt and pepper a little at a time until the seasonings are to your liking.

5 Serve the stew
As the meat will have fallen off the bone during the braising process, use tongs to carefully remove any bones before serving. Spoon the stew into the warmed bowls and garnish with the thyme leaves. Serve right away.

4 lb (2 kg) round red potatoes

2 teaspoons kosher salt

3 pinches freshly ground pepper

3 teaspoons fresh thyme leaves

4 cups (14 oz/440 g) sliced sweet onions such as Walla Walla or Vidalia

3 or 4 carrots, peeled and cut on the diagonal into slices ¼ inch (6 mm) thick

2 lb (1 kg) lamb stew meat such as leg, shoulder, or neck, preferably with some bone, cut into 1½–2-inch (4–5-cm) chunks

2 cups (16 fl oz/500 ml) boiling water

Leaves from 4–6 sprigs fresh thyme

MAKES 4–6 SERVINGS

CHEF'S TIP
Small red potatoes are often referred to as "new potatoes," and some supermarkets even label them that way. However, new potatoes are actually immature boiling potatoes of any variety. They are newly harvested, have thin skin, and will not keep long. True new potatoes are best suited for roasting, grilling, and salads.

Chili con Carne

A combination of chopped fresh chiles, chili powder, ground spices, and tomatoes gives this Texas-style chili a complex, robust flavor that continues to deepen during the long, slow cooking. The liquid should be nicely thickened by the time the chili is served, and the meat should be very tender but still have a little texture.

1 jalapeño chile

1 serrano chile

1 poblano chile

1 small red bell pepper (capsicum), stemmed and seeded (page 36)

2 lb (1 kg) well-marbled boneless beef chuck, fat trimmed, cut into 1/3–1/2-inch (9–12-mm) cubes and patted dry

2 teaspoons kosher salt

1/4 teaspoon freshly ground pepper

2 tablespoons canola oil

8 cloves garlic, minced (page 33)

4 teaspoons chili powder

1 teaspoon ground cumin

1/2 teaspoon ground coriander

1 can (28 oz/875 g) plum (Roma) tomatoes, with their juices, finely chopped in a food processor

1 teaspoon dried oregano

2 cups (16 fl oz/500 ml) Beef Stock (page 20) or water

1 cup (8 oz/250 g) sour cream, optional

12 sprigs fresh cilantro (fresh coriander)

MAKES 4–6 SERVINGS

CHEF'S TIP
Chili purists, especially in Texas (where chili was invented), believe that true chili never contains beans. Chili con carne literally means "with meat."

1 Prepare the chiles and pepper
If you prefer a mild chili, remove the seeds and ribs from the chiles, as they carry most of the heat, and then chop the chiles finely. Measure out 1/2 cup (4 oz/125 g) of the mixed chiles and set aside. For more details on working with chiles, turn to page 36. Dice the bell pepper.

2 Brown the beef
If you are not sure how to brown beef, turn to page 41. Sprinkle the meat cubes evenly with 1 teaspoon of the salt and 1/8 teaspoon of the pepper. Place a large, heavy frying pan over medium heat and add 1 tablespoon of the canola oil. When the surface of the oil appears to shimmer, add the beef cubes in batches and brown them on all sides, about 5 minutes for each batch. Do not crowd the pan, or the meat will steam instead of brown, and adjust the heat as necessary to sear the meat immediately on contact. As each batch is browned, use a slotted spoon to transfer it to a small Dutch oven or other heavy-bottomed pot.

3 Cook the vegetables
Add the remaining 1 tablespoon canola oil to the frying pan over medium heat. When the surface of the oil appears to shimmer, add the chiles, bell pepper, and garlic and cook, stirring, until the vegetables have softened and are beginning to turn golden, about 5 minutes. Stir in the chili powder, cumin, and coriander and cook for about 1 minute to develop the flavor of the spices. Add the tomatoes, oregano, and the remaining 1 teaspoon salt and 1/8 teaspoon pepper, stirring well to scrape up the browned bits from the pan bottom.

4 Simmer the chili
Add the vegetable mixture to the Dutch oven with the beef. Place the Dutch oven over medium heat, add the stock, and bring to a gentle boil, stirring occasionally. As soon as you see large bubbles begin to form, reduce the heat until only small bubbles occasionally break the surface. Cover the pot and cook until the meat is very tender and the liquid is slightly thickened, about 2 1/2 hours. If the chili seems too soupy, uncover it for the last 30 minutes to evaporate some of the liquid. About 10 minutes before you plan to serve the chili, preheat the oven to 200°F (95°C) and place individual bowls in the oven to warm.

5 Adjust the seasonings and serve the chili
Taste the chili; it should be quite boldly spiced, but if you feel the flavors are a little dull, stir in a bit more salt or pepper. Spoon the chili into the warmed bowls and top with the sour cream and cilantro sprigs. Serve right away.

Pasta & Bean Stew

This traditional Italian stew calls for a trio of pantry staples—dried beans, canned tomatoes, and pasta—and then brightens their flavors with fresh vegetables and tangy cheese. Nearly any small pasta shape, such as *tubetti* or elbow macaroni, can be used, but I like the chewy character that *orecchiette*, or "little ears," impart to it.

1 Soak the beans
Place the beans in a large sieve and rinse thoroughly under running cold water. Pick over to remove any stones or discolored beans. Place in a bowl, add cold water to cover by 2 inches (5 cm), and let soak overnight in the refrigerator.

2 Cook the beans
Drain the beans, place in a saucepan, and add water to cover by ½ inch (12 mm). Place over high heat and use a large spoon to skim off any foam that forms on the surface. As soon as you see large bubbles begin to form, reduce the heat until only small bubbles occasionally break the surface of the liquid, cover partially, and simmer until the beans are very soft, 1½–2 hours. Remove the pan from the heat and pour the beans into a sieve placed over a 4-cup (32–fl oz/1-l) glass measuring cup. Reserve the beans and their liquid separately.

3 Cook the vegetables
Place a Dutch oven over medium-low heat and add the olive oil. When the oil appears to shimmer, add the onion and cook, stirring, until the onion has softened, about 5 minutes. Add the garlic and cook for 1 minute to release its aroma. Crush the tomatoes with your hand and add them to the pot. Stir in the red pepper flakes. (If you know you will want this dish spicy, add an extra pinch of the pepper flakes.) Add enough stock to the reserved bean cooking liquid to total 3 cups (24 fl oz/750 ml) and then add the liquid and the reserved beans to the vegetables along with the salt and black pepper.

4 Cook the pasta and chard
Raise the heat to high and bring to a boil. When large bubbles appear on the surface of the liquid, add the pasta to the pot and reduce the heat to maintain the large bubbles. Cook, uncovered, until the pasta is almost tender, about 15 minutes for the orecchiette and 8–10 minutes for a smaller pasta such as *tubetti*. Stir the chard into the soup, reduce the heat to maintain small bubbles, and cook until the chard is tender, about 10 minutes. Meanwhile, preheat the oven to 200°F (95°C) and place individual bowls in the oven to warm. Add additional stock or water, ½ cup (4 fl oz/125 ml) at a time, if the mixture is too thick. It should be more stewlike than soupy.

5 Adjust the seasonings and serve the stew
Taste the stew. If it tastes dull, add more salt, black pepper, or red pepper flakes a little at a time until the seasonings are to your liking. Ladle the stew into the warmed bowls and serve right away. Pass the grated cheese at the table.

1 cup (7 oz/220 g) dried cannellini beans

¼ cup (2 fl oz/60 ml) extra-virgin olive oil

½ yellow onion, halved through the root end and then thinly sliced into half-moons

2 cloves garlic, minced (page 33)

1 cup (6 oz/185 g) drained canned plum (Roma) tomatoes

¼ teaspoon red pepper flakes

About 2 cups (16 fl oz/500 ml) Chicken Stock (page 18) or water

1 teaspoon kosher salt

⅛ teaspoon freshly ground black pepper

1 cup (5 oz/155 g) orecchiette or other small pasta shape

1 bunch Swiss chard, about ¾ lb (375 g), stems removed and leaves coarsely chopped (about 4 cups/8 oz/250 g)

1 cup (4 oz/125 g) freshly grated Parmigiano-Reggiano cheese

MAKES 4–6 SERVINGS

CHEF'S TIP
Many soups and stews are often better the day after they are made. If they contain starchy ingredients, such as pasta, beans, or potatoes, you may need to thin them with additional stock or water when reheating.

Using Key Tools & Equipment

Fortunately for beginners, the equipment for making soups and stews is straightforward. You'll find that the pots and pans and other kitchen gear you need to make these everyday dishes will serve you well for all kinds of cooking. The same ample pan you need for stock making is also ideal for boiling pasta. A blender or food processor performs dozens of preparation tasks. And every kitchen needs a basic assortment of sharp, well-balanced knives.

Pots & Pans

Three important elements should be considered when you select pots and pans for making soups and stews: size, shape, and material. The best pan for simmering stock is taller than it is wide. This narrow shape means that there is less surface area, so the liquid doesn't evaporate as readily.

However, when you brown ingredients, as you do in slowly caramelizing onions for French Onion Soup (page 55), a broad saucepan with greater surface is desirable. Some stews such as Chili con Carne (page 128), start with browning beef cubes and vegetables in a large, heavy frying pan. Other stews, especially those that are finished in the oven like Irish Lamb Stew (page 127), work best in a Dutch oven, a deep, wide, pan with a lid and a heavy base. This versatile pan can be used for both browning meat and simmering liquids.

For making the roux that thickens Cream of Broccoli Soup (page 93) and other cream soups, use a heavy saucepan large enough to accommodate the entire quantity of soup (more than 1½ qt/1.5 l), allowing plenty of room to stir the bubbling mixture. Be sure your kitchen includes a collapsible steamer basket for cooking vegetables, and a large roasting pan for browning the meat bones and vegetables to make browned beef stock.

Slow and steady cooking produces the best soups and stews and calls for pots and pans with heavy, solid walls that hold heat well and cook foods evenly without scorching. When shopping, look for materials that are good heat conductors. Possibilities include stainless steel, anodized aluminum, brushed aluminum

and porcelain-coated cast iron, as well as such combinations as stainless steel–lined anodized aluminum.

Each material has advantages for certain types of cooking. For example, pans lined with stainless steel, enamel, or porcelain will not react with acidic ingredients such as tomatoes or wine, avoiding the metallic taste that results when cooking in reactive materials such as nonanodized aluminum. An expert cookware dealer can advise you which variety is best suited for your cooking needs and budget.

Basic Cutlery

The two kinds of knives most commonly used for making soups and stews are a 4-inch (10-cm) paring knife for peeling and trimming vegetables and an 8- to 10-inch (20- to 24-cm) chef's knife for chopping, dicing and slicing (the measurement is the blade length). High-carbon steel knives are a wise investment, as they are crafted for a lifetime of frequent use. A thin boning knife can help separate chicken pieces if you need to cut the bird up before poaching. Kitchen scissors come in handy for snipping herbs or cutting clams for chowder. When using any knife, be sure to cut ingredients on a heavy wooden or plastic cutting board. To keep the boards from moving around on the counter as you work, place a folded damp paper towel or kitchen towel under the board.

Measuring Supplies

To be sure of accurate measurements, have on hand both dry and liquid measuring cups and a set of measuring spoons. In soup making, it is useful if the liquid measuring cup is made of heatproof glass and has a spout.

Whisks, Spoons & Skimmers

Stirring a thickened soup is simpler when you use a wire whisk. Choose one that's big enough to easily swirl around a deep pan. Long-handled wooden and metal spoons are needed for stirring and mixing, and a perforated skimmer or slotted spoon is good for skimming simmering stocks and removing bones and other solids from stocks and soups.

Ladles

Ladles in various sizes and capacities are a must for serving soups. You'll use ladles for safely and efficiently moving soup mixtures to a blender or food processor for puréeing. Ladles also come in handy when transferring stock to a sieve placed over a bowl for straining. The most versatile sizes for home use are 2 oz (60 ml) and 4 oz (125 ml) capacities.

Puréeing Equipment

Throughout this book, various types of equipment are recommended for puréeing soups and sauces. Each has a slightly different function. A food processor is the most versatile, as it is good at transforming cooked vegetables into a purée or a more complex mixture into a smooth soup. If your processor work bowl isn't large, you may need to process in small batches. You can use a stand blender for some of these tasks, as well; work with limited quantities, filling the container only half full, to prevent hot mixtures from flowing out the top. A blender will aerate a rich soup mixture, giving it a more delicate consistency.

A hand-operated food mill may appear to be an old-fashioned tool. But a non-reactive stainless-steel version is now available, and it's still the best way to purée

the solids for Bouillabaisse (page 119). A more recent kitchen development is the immersion blender (stick blender). With this device you can purée a simple vegetable soup by slowly moving the wand around in a deep pot.

Tongs & Spatulas

Chefs make frequent use of stainless-steel tongs, and you'll find them helpful when you need to turn browning chunks of meat. A durable heatproof silicone or metal spatula is also a must. You'll use either to scrape pans when deglazing. The former can be used to coax the last bit of a puréed soup out of a food processor or blender.

Straining & Bundling Supplies

Cheesecloth (muslin)—look for it in the notions aisle of the supermarket

or hardware store—and cotton kitchen string are invaluable when you make soups and stews. You'll need them both to bundle herbs for a bouquet garni, and you'll use the cheesecloth for straining stocks. A collection of fine-mesh sieves is a must for straining stocks, as well.

Mixing Bowls

You can never have too many mixing bowls. You'll pour strained stocks into large bowls and use smaller ones to hold prepped ingredients. Look for tempered-glass and stainless-steel bowls that can be used for hot mixtures and will not react with acidic ingredients.

Serving Equipment

Once your soup or stew is ready, you will want to ladle it into attractive serving dishes. A soup tureen is a beautiful and

traditional choice, but it is not the only option. You can ladle your soup directly into warmed bowls in the kitchen and carry them to the table.

You'll find bowls in various styles and shapes, but size is more important. If you are serving soup as a first course, you will want a small serving—in a small bowl. A bisque or other smooth, elegant soup might be served in the small, round soup dish called a bisque cup. Soups served as a main course are ladled out in more generous portions in larger bowls. When you bring soup bowls to the table, place them on liner plates so guests have a place to set their spoons. On casual occasions, however, soup tastes just as good sipped from oversized mugs.

Stews can also be presented more than one way. If you're pairing a stew with potatoes or rice, as you might when serving Beef & Red Wine Stew (page 124), you can use either wide, deep plates or wide, shallow bowls. Meal-in-one stews like Chicken, Shrimp & Andouille Gumbo (page 113) call for wide, deep bowls to accommodate the rich variety of ingredients they contain.

Graters, Raspers & Peelers

Small wonders as graters, reamers, raspers, and peelers perform countless useful tasks and should be standard equipment in any kitchen. When you grate onion and shred cheese for Cheddar Cheese Soup (page 108), a box grater-shredder is essential. More sophisticated rasp graters, with rasps ranging in size from fine to coarse, are ideal for grating and shredding everything from citrus peels and fresh ginger to hard cheese. A citrus zester makes garnish-perfect strands in seconds.

And you can make light work of peeling potatoes, asparagus, and carrots with a vegetable peeler.

Oven Mitts & Pot Holders

Handling hot cookware and serving dishes calls for a supply of thick pot holders and oven mitts. In a pinch, you can grab a thick towel to protect your hands. However, it can be a dangerous strategy around an open flame, so be careful when using them.

Storage Supplies

Sometimes you will make more stock, soup, or stew than you can use right away, and you will need something in which to store it. Plastic containers with tight-fitting lids are good for both freezer and refrigerator use. Use press-on labels to keep track of the date and contents.

Glossary

ANDOUILLE SAUSAGE A spicy pork sausage that is a staple of Cajun cooking, andouille is available at many supermarkets and delicatessens. Kielbasa, a Polish sausage, may be substituted.

BEANS, DRIED
Dried beans are a practical, economical food with a long shelf life, keeping for a year when stored airtight in a cool, dry cupboard.

Black Small and uniformly black with a shiny surface. Used widely in Latin American cooking to make soups and dips.

Borlotti Rosy-beige bean with maroon speckles; used in Italian cooking.

Cannellini Ivory-colored bean with a smooth texture. Popular in salads, side dishes, and soups, including classic Italian minestrone.

Chickpea Also known as the garbanzo bean, a rich, nutty-flavored, large beige bean with a firm texture.

Great Northern Also called simply white beans, these small, oval-shaped beans can be used in place of other small white beans, such as navy or white kidney. They have a mild flavor and creamy texture.

Lentils Small and flat, lentils may be green, brown, yellow, pink, or black. Mild flavored and quick cooking, they are very versatile.

Split peas Small, pale green or yellow dried legumes. Split peas cook quickly and are best known as the basis for split pea soup.

White kidney Sometimes mistaken for cannellini, this mild-flavored variety is often used in Italian dishes and is an acceptable substitute for cannellini beans in most recipes.

BEARD The little tuft of fibers a mussel uses to connect to rocks or pilings. To remove it, cut and scrape it with a small sharp knife or sturdy scissors. You may also pull it sharply down toward the hinged point of the shells with your fingers until it breaks off.

BONES FOR STOCK In making meat stock, two kinds of bones are desirable: soup bones, which are typically leg and knuckle bones,

and bony cuts from the neck or shin with meat still attached. The shin (or shank), which is the lower leg, is a naturally well-exercised muscle on any animal. The meat is flavorful and succulent and adds delicious flavor to stock with long, slow cooking. Soup bones are not meaty but are rich in gelatin and marrow, the soft, rich, nutritious tissue lodged in the hollow center of bones, which give character to stock.

CELERY ROOT Also known as celeriac, celery root is a knobbly, round winter vegetable with a subtle celery flavor.

CHEESES
Visiting a good cheese shop is a rewarding experience, since you're able to taste the cheeses before you buy. Wrap cheeses in waxed paper or parchment (baking) paper rather than plastic wrap so they can breathe, and store them in the crisper drawer of the refrigerator, which has the optimum temperature and humidity level.

Cheddar First made in the village of Cheddar in England, this cheese is appreciated for its tangy, salty flavor, which ranges from mild to sharp, depending on age. Although naturally a creamy white, Cheddar is often dyed orange with annatto, a paste made from achiote seeds.

Gruyère This semifirm, dense, smooth cow's milk cheese is produced in Switzerland and France and is appreciated for its mild, nutty flavor and superior melting properties.

Parmigiano-Reggiano Produced in the Emilia-Romagna region of Italy, Parmigiano-Reggiano is true Parmesan. Look for an aged, firm cheese with a pale yellow to medium straw color and a piquant, slightly salty flavor. To be certain you are getting the highest quality, look for "Parmigiano-Reggiano" stenciled vertically on the rind.

CHILES
Fresh chiles range in size from tiny to large, in heat intensity from mild to fiery hot, and in use from seasoning to a vegetable. Select firm, bright-colored chiles with blemish-free skins. To reduce the hotness of a chile,

remove the ribs and seeds, where the heat-producing compound, called *capsaicin*, resides. When working with hot chiles, wear gloves to avoid burning your skin, then wash your hands and any utensils thoroughly with hot, soapy water the moment you finish.

Chipotle A dried and smoked jalapeño chile, with lots of flavor and lots of heat. These dark brown chiles are about 4 inches (10 cm) long and are sold dried or in cans or jars in an oniony tomato mixture called adobo sauce.

Jalapeño The jalapeño measures from 2 to 4 inches (5 to 10 cm) long, has a generous amount of flesh, and ranges from mildly hot to fiery. Green jalapeños are widely available, but you can sometimes find red ones, the ripened form, which are slightly sweeter.

Poblano Large and fairly mild, the fresh dark green poblano is about 5 inches (13 cm) long and has broad "shoulders." Poblanos, which are usually roasted and peeled, have a nutty flavor and are often stuffed for chiles rellenos. When dried, poblanos are called ancho chiles.

Serrano The serrano is similar to the familiar jalapeño in heat intensity and appearance, although it is smaller, usually about 2 inches (5 cm) long, and more slender. It can be green or red.

CLAMS
The clam is one of the most versatile members of the shellfish family. When added to soups and stews, those dishes benefit from the clams' fresh, clean, sweet flavor. Buy the freshest clams you can find from a reputable fish merchant. They are sold live in the shell or freshly shucked and packed in pint (500 ml) and quart (1 l) containers that usually contain clam liquor (or liquid), too.

Cherrystone A small hard-shelled Atlantic clam, measuring up to 3 inches (7.5 cm) in diameter.

Littleneck There are two kinds available on the market. The smallest of the hard-shelled clam family, Atlantic littlenecks measure 1½–2¼ inches (4–6 cm) in diameter. These are particularly sweet and delicious raw or very gently cooked. Pacific littlenecks, which are harvested from Mexico to Alaska, are also known as Pacific clams and are about the same size.

CRABMEAT When a recipe calls for crabmeat, the easiest solution is to seek out fresh lump crabmeat sold at fish markets. It yields the sweetest, moistest meat. If unavailable, use good-quality frozen crabmeat that has been thoroughly thawed and well drained before chopping. Avoid imitation crabmeat, or surimi, which is made from pollack or other white-fleshed fish.

CREAM, HEAVY Cream that contains between 36 and 40 percent fat; when used in a sauce, it can be boiled without separating. Heavy cream is also called double cream in Britain, and it may also be labeled heavy whipping cream or just whipping cream in the United States. Look for cream that has been pasteurized but not ultrapasteurized.

CRÈME FRAÎCHE A soured, cultured cream product, originally from France, crème fraîche is similar to sour cream. Silken and thick, it is tangy and sweet, with a subtle, nutty flavor. Crème fraîche loses its flavor as it sits, so buy it as fresh as possible.

CUCUMBER, ENGLISH Also called hothouse cucumbers, these cucumbers can grow up to 2 feet (60 cm) long. They are nearly seedless, which makes them a popular choice for gazpacho.

CUMIN This spice comes from the seeds of a member of the parsley family and has a distinct aroma and a nutty, smoky flavor when added to soups and stews.

CURRY POWDER Typical ingredients of this spice blend from South Asia can have up to twenty spices and might include turmeric, cumin, coriander, pepper, cinnamon, cloves, or ginger. Curry powders are usually categorized as mild, hot, and very hot. Madras curry powder is considered a well-balanced version with medium heat.

FENNEL The stems of the fennel plant swell to overlap at the base, forming a bulb with white to pale green ribbed layers that are similar to celery in appearance and texture. The green leaves are light and feathery and resemble dill. Fennel leaves, seeds, and stems all have a sweet flavor, faintly reminiscent of black licorice.

FENNEL SEEDS These beige, ridged seeds have a delicate anise flavor. Commonly used to season Italian sausages, they are a classic ingredient in French seafood stews.

GINGER A refreshing combination of spicy and sweet in both aroma and flavor, ginger adds a lively note to soups and stews. Hard and knobby fresh ginger has thin, pale brown skin. Although called a root, it is actually a rhizome, or underground stem. Select fresh ginger that is firm and heavy with smooth, unbroken skin.

HALF-AND-HALF There are many varieties of cream, all categorized according to the amount of milk fat in the mixture. Half-and-half, or half cream, is mixture of equal parts milk and cream and is 10 to 12 percent milk fat. Half-and-half cannot be whipped.

HERBS
Learning to use fresh herbs is an excellent way to improve your cooking. Dried herbs have their place, of course, but fresh herbs typically bring brighter flavors to soups, stews and other dishes.

Basil Used in kitchens throughout the Mediterranean and in Southeast Asia, basil adds a highly aromatic, peppery flavor.

Bay leaves These elongated gray-green leaves, used to flavor sauces, soups, stews, and braises, impart a slightly sweet, citrusy, nutty flavor. Usually sold dried, bay leaves, which are leathery and can have sharp edges, should be removed from a dish before serving.

Chives The slender, bright green stems of chives are used to give an onionlike flavor without the bite; they taste more like a delicate and sweet green (spring) onion. Chives can be snipped with kitchen scissors to any length and used to garnish soups.

Cilantro Also called fresh coriander and Chinese parsley, cilantro is a strongly flavored herb used extensively in Mexican, Asian, Indian, Latin, and Middle Eastern cuisines. Cilantro's pungent aniselike aroma and bright astringent taste are distinctive. Use it sparingly at first until you are familiar with its flavor. When shopping, do not confuse cilantro and flat-leaf (Italian) parsley, which have leaves that closely resemble one another. Always use fresh cilantro, as it loses its flavor when dried.

Dill Fine, feathery leaves with a distinct aromatic flavor, dill is often used in savory pastries and baked vegetables, but it also pairs well with soups and stews.

Marjoram This Mediterranean herb is a slightly milder cousin to oregano. Marjoram has a delicate floral flavor that complements many soups.

Oregano Aromatic, pungent, and spicy, this herb, also known as wild marjoram, is used fresh or dried as a seasoning in all kinds of savory dishes. Oregano is especially delicious in tomato-based soups.

Parsley, flat-leaf Also called Italian parsley, this faintly peppery herb adds vibrant color and pleasing flavor to many soups and stews. It is far more flavorful than the curly-leaf type.

Sage A popular Italian herb with soft, gray-green leaves that are pungent and aromatic. Used fresh or dried, sage brings an earthiness to bean-based or meat-based soups and stews.

Tarragon With its slender, deep green leaves and elegant, slightly aniselike scent, tarragon is a popular addition to soups.

Thyme Tiny green leaves on thin stems, this herb is a mild, all-purpose seasoning. Its floral, earthy flavor complements soups and stews as well as many other dishes. If a large amount is needed, gently pull the leaves backward off the stem with one motion. When the thyme stems are young and still very soft, you can chop them along with the leaves, but more mature stems will be woody and should be discarded.

HOT-PEPPER SAUCE A splash of hot-pepper sauce adds a bright flavor to soups. There are countless varieties of hot-pepper sauce made in a rainbow of colors and a range of heat levels. Try several brands until you find one you especially like.

LEEK A sweet and mild-flavored member of the onion family, leeks are long and cylindrical with pale white root ends and dark green leaves. The green leaves are tough; only the white and sometimes the light green parts are used in most recipes. Select firm, unblemished leeks, small to medium in size. Leeks have a buttery taste when cooked.

LINGUIÇA SAUSAGE A highly-seasoned Portuguese pork sausage flavored with garlic and onions.

LOBSTER Fresh lobster meat is preferred for soups and stews, but if you lack a reliable source, frozen lobster tails, usually from spiny lobsters, and precooked whole lobster are acceptable substitutes.

MADEIRA A fortified wine from Portugal, Madeira ranges in color and flavor from light, nutty, and dry aperitif wines to darker, sweet after-dinner wines. Madeira enhances both sweet and savory dishes, especially rich stews and soups.

MATZOH MEAL Also spelled matzo, this meal, ground from brittle, unleavened matzoh bread, is used for making matzoh balls, among other preparations.

MUSHROOMS Almost forty thousand varieties of mushroom exist in the world, but only a fraction of them make it to the table, where they are enjoyed for their rich, earthy flavor. These are some of the more common varieties.

Button Also called white mushroom, this cultivated all-purpose mushroom is readily found in grocery stores.

Cremini Also known as common brown, Italian, or Roman mushrooms, these small, pale brown, cultivated specimens mature to become portobellos.

Shiitake The most popular mushrooms in Japan and now widely cultivated throughout the world. Buff to dark brown, fresh shiitakes should have smooth, plump caps.

MUSSELS A saltwater mollusk with slightly pointed shells ranging in color from blue-green to black, mussels have cream to orange-colored meat that is sweeter than that of oysters or clams when used in a soup or stew.

MUSTARD POWDER Mustard seeds come in three colors: white (also called yellow), brown, and black. The white seeds are the mildest, followed in pungency by brown or black. Look for English mustard powder, which is a classic blend of ground white and brown seeds sometimes mixed with wheat flour for bulk and turmeric for color.

NONREACTIVE A term used to describe a pan or dish made of or lined with a material that will not react with acidic ingredients. This includes stainless steel, enamel, ceramic, and glass.

NUTMEG The seed of a tropical evergreen tree, a nutmeg is about ¾ inch (2 cm) long with a hard shell. This warm, slightly sweet spice should be bought whole and then freshly grated on the finest rasps of a nutmeg or similar grater just before using. Nutmeg is often used to season creamy soups.

OIL

Cooking oils, fats that are liquid at room temperature, play an essential role in the kitchen. A recipe's other ingredients and its heat requirements usually will suggest which oil is most appropriate to use. As a general rule, choose less refined, more flavorful oils for uncooked uses, and refined, less flavorful oils for coating foods and cooking.

Asian sesame Pressed from toasted sesame seeds, this deep amber-colored oil has a rich, nutty flavor. It is used sparingly as a seasoning.

Canola This neutral-flavored oil, appreciated for its healthful monounsaturated fats, is recommended for general cooking.

Olive Olive oil contributes a delicate, fruity flavor to dishes. Deeply flavorful extra-virgin olive oil is produced from the first press of olives without heat or chemicals. Virgin and pure olive oils, products of subsequent pressings, are good, less-expensive cooking oils that add subtle flavor.

OKRA Indispensable to a good gumbo, okra are slender, ridged green seedpods with pointed ends. During cooking, the cut pods release a viscous substance that thickens the gumbo.

ONIONS
These root vegetables, in the same family as leeks and garlic, are some of the most common ingredients in the kitchen.

Green Also known as scallions or spring onions, green onions are the immature shoots of the bulb onion, with a narrow white base that has not yet begun to swell and long, flat green leaves.

Sweet Some regions are known for growing sweet, mild onions that are excellent for cooking and eating raw. These include Maui from Hawaii, Walla Walla from Washington, and Vidalia from Georgia.

White These onions are more pungent than the red onion, but milder and less sweet than the yellow. Large and round or slightly flattened, white onions are sometimes called white Spanish onions.

Yellow Yellow globe onions are the common, all-purpose onion sold in supermarkets. They can be globular, flattened, or slightly elongated and has parchmentlike golden brown skin.

ORECCHIETTE Small, indented, circular pasta. The name, which means "little ears" in Italian, refers to the shape of the pasta.

ORZO Taking its name from the Italian word for barley, orzo is a small pasta shaped much like large grains of rice.

PANCETTA This flavorful unsmoked Italian bacon, which derives its name from *pancia*, the Italian word for "belly," has a moist, silky texture. It is made by rubbing a slab of pork belly with a mixture of spices that may include cinnamon, cloves, or juniper berries, then rolling the slab into a tight cylinder and curing it for at least 2 months.

PAPRIKA Made from ground dried red peppers, paprika is used both as a garnish and as a flavoring. The flavor can range from sweet and mild to hot. Sweet paprika is the most commonly used.

PARSNIP A relative of the carrot, this ivory-colored root closely resembles its brighter, more familiar cousin. Parsnips have a slightly sweet flavor and a tough, starchy texture that softens with cooking.

PEARL BARLEY Barley is a grain with a nutty flavor and chewy texture that lends itself well to soups and side dishes. It is most often found in the common pearled form, meaning hulled and polished to a pearl-like shape and sheen.

PESTO A puréed Italian sauce most classically made of fresh basil, garlic, pine nuts, olive oil, and grated aged Italian cheese.

RED PEPPER FLAKES The red flakes and yellow seeds of slender dried red chiles, red pepper flakes are a popular seasoning in Italy. Just a pinch or two will add a touch of heat to many soups and stews.

SAFFRON The stigma of a small crocus, saffron is a highly aromatic spice that tints food a bright yellow. Buy saffron threads in small quantities and store them in a cool, dark place. As powdered saffron loses its flavor more quickly than do the threads, crush the threads only as you need them.

SALT Table salt is usually amended with iodine and with additives that enable it to flow freely. kosher salt, which is usually free of additives, has large, coarse flakes that are easy to grasp with your fingertips. It is also used more liberally than regular table salt or sea salt because it does not taste as salty. If you prefer kosher salt, keep in mind that you'll need almost twice as much.

SHALLOTS These small members of the onion family look like large cloves of garlic covered with papery bronze or reddish skin. Shallots have white flesh streaked with purple, a crisp texture, and a flavor more subtle than that of onions. They are often used for flavoring recipes that would be overpowered by the stronger taste of onion.

SHERRY A fortified Spanish wine now also made elsewhere, sherry ranges from dry and light to sweet and heavy and from pale to deep amber. It can be used to add flavor to soups, usually at the end of cooking. Look for medium-dry sherry for general cooking.

SNOW PEAS Also called mangetouts, these flat, wide bright green peas are eaten pod and all. Choose crisp, vivid green pods concealing tiny peas.

SOY SAUCE This pungent, salty sauce, made from fermented soy beans, wheat, and water, comes in various types and textures. Soy sauce ranges from light and mild to deep, dark, and intense. Reduced-sodium soy sauce, while still high in sodium, has about half the sodium of regular soy sauce, allowing the cook more control over the seasoning of a dish.

SQUASH, BUTTERNUT This large winter squash has beige skin and orange-yellow flesh. It is identifiable by the round bulb at one end. When roasted, its flavorful, dense flesh makes a velvety soup.

SWEET BAGUETTE A French bread that's been formed into a long, narrow cylindrical loaf. It usually has a crisp brown crust and light, chewy interior. Called "sweet" to differentiate it from a sourdough loaf.

SWISS CHARD A leafy cooking green with large, crinkled leaves on fleshy, ribbed stems. There are two common varieties: one with red stems and another with pearly white stems. Red chard, also marketed as rhubarb or ruby chard, has a slightly earthier flavor, while chard with white or yellow stems tends to be sweeter.

TOMATO PASTE A dense purée made from slow-cooked tomatoes that have been strained and cooked down to a deep red concentrate. It has a low acid and high sugar content and is sold in tubes, tins, and jars. After opening, store in the refrigerator.

TOMATOES, PLUM These egg-shaped tomatoes, also known as Roma tomatoes, have a meaty, flavorful flesh. When buying plum tomatoes, choose specimens that are fragrant. For canned plum tomatoes or those packaged in aseptic boxes, look for brands low in sodium and other additives. Canned San Marzano tomatoes, imported from Italy, often promise the best quality.

TUBETTINI These small, stout pasta "tubes" are hearty additions to soups and stews.

TURNIP The common turnip is a root vegetable with crisp white flesh and white skin with a purple cap, although some varieties have yellow flesh and the cap might be green, red, white, or even black. Young turnips are tender and have a mild, sweet flavor. The flavor grows stronger and the flesh woodier with age.

VINEGARS
Many types are available, made from a variety of red or white wines or, like cider vinegar and rice vinegar, from fruits and grains. Vinegars are further seasoned by infusing them with fresh herbs, fruit, garlic, or other flavorful ingredients.

Balsamic An aged vinegar made from the unfermented grape juice of white Trebbiano grapes. Balsamic may be aged briefly, for only 1 year, or for 75 years or longer. The vinegar slowly evaporates and grows sweeter and mellower. Balsamic vinegar is a specialty of Italy's Emilia-Romagna region, chiefly the town of Modena.

Red wine This pantry staple is carried in most supermarkets. Better-quality varietal wine vinegars are available in specialty-food stores.

Rice Produced from fermented rice and widely used in Asian cuisines, rice vinegar adds a slight acidity to soups and other cooked dishes. Look for unseasoned rice vinegar.

WAX BEANS Long beans with the same characteristics as green beans, but pale or medium yellow in color.

WHITE PEPPER Made from black peppercorns that have had their skins removed before the berries are dried, white pepper is often less aromatic and more mild in flavor than black pepper. It is favored in the preparation of light-colored puréed soups.

ZEST The colored portion of citrus rind, which is rich in flavorful oils. The white portion of the rind, called the pith, is bitter. Pesticides concentrate in the skins of fruits and vegetables, so look for organic fruits when choosing citrus intended for zesting.

Index

ƒP

FREE PRESS

A Division of Simon & Schuster, Inc.
1230 Avenue of the Americas
New York, NY 10020

WILLIAMS-SONOMA

Founder & Vice-Chairman Chuck Williams

WELDON OWEN INC.

Chief Executive Officer John Owen
President and Chief Operating Officer Terry Newell
Chief Financial Officer Christine E. Munson
Vice President International Sales Stuart Laurence
Creative Director Gaye Allen
Publisher Hannah Rahill
Senior Editor Jennifer Newens
Editor Stephanie V. W. Lucianovic
Editorial Assistant Juli Vendzules
Art Director Kyrie Forbes
Designers Marisa Kwek and Adrienne Aquino
Production Director Chris Hemesath
Color Manager Teri Bell
Production and Reprint Coordinator Todd Rechner
Food Stylist William Smith
Prop Stylist Marina Malchin
Assistant Food Stylist Matthew Vohr
Assistant Food Stylist and Hand Model Brittany Williams
Photographer's Assistant Mario Jimenez

PHOTO CREDITS

Jeff Kauck, all photography, except the following:
Bill Bettencourt: Pages 10–11,
33 (leeks sequence), 42 (blender sequence), and 129.
Mark Thomas: Pages 32, 33 (garlic sequence), 133 (top middle),
134 (bottom right), and 135 (bottom right).

THE MASTERING SERIES

Conceived and produced by Weldon Owen Inc.
814 Montgomery Street, San Francisco, CA 94133
Telephone: 415 291 0100 Fax: 415 291 8841

In collaboration with Williams-Sonoma, Inc.
3250 Van Ness Avenue, San Francisco, CA 94109

A WELDON OWEN PRODUCTION
Copyright © 2005 by Weldon Owen Inc. and Williams-Sonoma Inc.

All rights reserved, including the right of reproduction in whole or in part
in any form.

FREE PRESS and colophon are registered trademarks of Simon & Schuster, Inc.

For information regarding special discounts for bulk purchases,
please contact Simon & Schuster Special Sales at 1 800 456 6798 or
business@simonandschuster.com

Set in ITC Berkeley and FF The Sans.

Color separations by Embassy Graphics.
Printed and bound in China by SNP Leefung Printers Limited.

First printed in 2005.

10 9 8 7 6 5 4 3 2 1

Library of Congress Cataloging-in-Publication data is available.

ISBN–13: 978-0-7432-6736-6
ISBN–10: 0-7432-6736-2

ACKNOWLEDGMENTS

Weldon Owen wishes to thank the following people for their generous support
in producing this book: Desne Ahlers, Andy Anderson, Alison Attenborough,
Carrie Bradley, Ken DellaPenta, Emily Jahn, Ashley Johnson, Karen Kemp,
Shana Lopes, Jessica Newens, Deborah Lawrence Schafer, Cynthia Scheer,
Sharon Silva, Bob Simmons, and Coleen Simmons.

A NOTE ON WEIGHTS AND MEASURES

All recipes include customary U.S. and metric measurements. Metric conversions are based on
a standard developed for these books and have been rounded off. Actual weights may vary.